American Book Company
The Standards Experts

MW01503199

Dear Educator,

Thank you for your interest in American Book Company's state-specific test preparation resources. Enclosed you will find the preview book and/or demonstration disk that you requested. We commend you for your interest in pursuing your students' success. Feel free to contact us with any questions about our books, software, or the ordering process.

Our Products Feature	**Your Students Will Improve**
Multiple-choice diagnostic tests	Confidence and mastery of subjects
Step-by-step instruction	Concept development
Frequent practice exercises	Critical thinking
Chapter reviews	Test-taking skills
Multiple-choice practice tests	Problem-solving skills

About American Book Company

American Book Company's writers and curriculum specialists have **over 100 years of combined teaching experience**, working with students from kindergarten through middle, high school, and adult education.

Our company specializes in **test preparation books and software** for high school graduation tests and exit exams. We currently offer test preparation materials for Alabama, Arizona, California, Florida, Georgia, Indiana, Louisiana, Maine, Maryland, Minnesota, Mississippi, Nevada, New Jersey, North Carolina, Ohio, Oklahoma, South Carolina, Tennessee, and Texas.

We also offer books and software for **middle school review and high school remediation**. The materials in the Basics Made Easy Series are aligned with the standards for the Iowa Test of Basic Skills and the Stanford 9 Achievement Test.

While some other book publishers offer general test preparation materials, our student workbooks and software are **specifically designed** to meet the unique requirements of **each state's exit exam** or graduation test. Whether the subject is language arts, math, reading, science, social studies, or writing, our books and software are designed to meet the standards published by the state agency responsible for the graduation test or exit exam. Our materials provide **no tricks or secret solutions** to passing standardized tests, just engaging instruction and practical exercises to help students master the concepts and skills they need.

While we cannot guarantee success, our products are designed to provide students with the concept and skill development they need for the graduation test or exit exam in their own state. We look forward to hearing from you soon.

Sincerely,

Joe Wood
Curriculum Specialist

PO Box 2638 ★ Woodstock, GA 30188-1383 ★ Phone: 1-888-264-5877 ★ Fax: 1-866-827-3240
Web Site: www.americanbookcompany.com ★ E-mail: contact@americanbookcompany.com

MCA-II Grade 8 Reading
Chart of Standards

Passing the MCA-II Reading Grade 8 **Chart of Standards** **Strand I - Reading and Literature** The following chart correlates each question on the Diagnostic Test, Practice Test 1, and Practice Test 2 to the Minnesota English and Language Arts curriculum competency goals ***standards and benchmarks published by the Minnesota Department of Education***. These test questions are also correlated with chapters in *Passing the Minnesota MCA-II Grade 8 Reading Test.*				
Competency Standards	**Chapter Number**	**Diagnostic Test Questions**	**Practice Test 1 Questions**	**Practice Test 2 Questions**
Sub-strand B. Vocabulary Expansion – The student will apply a variety of strategies to expand reading, listening, and speaking vocabularies				
I.B.2 and I.B.3 Students will determine the meaning of unknown words by using a dictionary or context clues. Students will recognize and interpret words with multiple meanings.	1	1, 9, 21, 26, 36, 41, 45	3, 6, 11, 23, 28, 33	3, 9, 13, 27, 31, 40
Sub-strand C. Comprehension – The student will understand the meaning of texts using a variety of strategies and will demonstrate literal, interpretive, inferential, and evaluative comprehension.				
I.C.1 Students will summarize and paraphrase main idea an supporting details.	2	2, 3, 8, 16, 18, 19, 23, 40, 42, 44	5, 8, 13, 16, 19, 22, 25, 27, 36, 39, 40, 48	1, 4, 7, 15, 18, 22, 25, 28, 30, 38, 48
I.C.4 Students will make inferences and draw conclusions based on explicit and implied information from text.	3	6, 10, 12, 20, 27, 28, 35, 38, 46, 47	2, 12, 21, 26, 31, 32, 34, 42, 44, 45	2, 6, 10, 12, 21, 36, 37, 43, 45

Contain Domain	Chapter Number	Diagnostic Test Questions	Practice Test 1 Questions	Practice Test 2 Questions
I.C.6 Students will evaluate the adequacy, accuracy, and appropriateness of the author's evidence in a persuasive text.	5	34	18, 41	42, 46
I.C.11 Students will distinguish fact from opinion in two selections on the same topic and give evidence.	4	4, 24, 43	1, 37	5, 35, 44
I.C.14 Students will critically read and evaluate to determine the author's purpose, point of view, audience, and message.	5, 6	17, 22, 39	4, 7, 15, 20, 24 35, 43, 47	8, 17, 33, 41, 47

Sub-strand D. Literature – The student will actively engage in the reading process and read, understand, respond to, analyze, interpret, evaluate, and appreciate a wide variety of fiction, poetic, and nonfiction texts.

Contain Domain	Chapter Number	Diagnostic Test Questions	Practice Test 1 Questions	Practice Test 2 Questions
I.D.3 Students will analyze a character's traits, emotions, or motivation and give supportive evidence from the text.	7	7, 13, 14	29, 30	14, 16, 19, 24
I.D.4 and **I.D.7** Students will analyze and evaluate how figurative language and literary devices contribute to the meaning of the text.	8	5, 11, 15, 31	10, 14, 17	11, 23, 26, 34
I.D.12 Students will respond to literature using ideas and details from the text to support reactions and make literary connections.	10	25, 32, 33, 37, 48	9, 38, 41, 46	16, 20, 29, 32, 39
I.C.1, I.C.4, I.C.6, I.C.11, I.C.14, I.D.3, I.D.4, I.D.7, I.D.12	9	8, 25, 40	9, 25, 41	16, 32, 48

American Book Company
The Standards Experts

PASSING THE MINNESOTA

8th Grade MCA-II

in

Reading

Mike Kabel
Zuzana Urbanek

Dr. Frank J. Pintozzi, Project Coordinator

American Book Company
PO Box 2638
Woodstock, GA 30188-1383
Toll Free: 1 (888) 264-5877   Phone: (770) 928-2834
Fax: (770) 928-7483   Toll Free Fax: 1 (866) 827-3240
Web site: www.americanbookcompany.com

ACKNOWLEDGEMENTS

The authors would like to gratefully acknowledge the formatting and technical contributions of Marsha Torrens.

This product/publication includes images from CorelDRAW 9 and 11 which are protected by the copyright laws of the United States, Canada, and elsewhere. Used under license.

Table of Contents

Chapter 10 Comparing and Contrasting   143

Practice Test 1   159

Practice Test 2   173

Index   189

Grade 8 MCA-II Reading Test
Preface

Passing The Grade 8 MCA-II Reading Test will help students who are learning or reviewing standards for the reading sections of the **Minnesota Comprehensive Assessment-II (MCA-II)** exams. The materials in this book are based on the MCA-II assessment standards as published by the Minnesota Department of Education.

This book contains several sections:

    1) General information about the book itself

    2) A pretest

    3) An evaluation chart

    4) Ten chapters that teach the concepts and skills needed for test readiness

    5) Two practice tests

Standards are posted at the beginning of each chapter, in the diagnostic and practice tests as well as in a chart included in the answer manual.

———————————————— ◄►————————————————

We welcome comments and suggestions about this book. Please contact the authors at

American Book Company
PO Box 2638
Woodstock, GA 30188-1383

Call Toll Free: (888) 264-5877
Phone: (770) 928-2834
Toll Free Fax: 1 (866) 827-3240

Visit us online at
www.americanbookcompany.com

About the Project Coordinator:

Dr. Frank J. Pintozzi has taught English and Reading at the high school and college levels for over 27 years. An adjunct professor of Reading and ESL at Kennesaw State University, he has authored eight textbooks on reading, writing strategies and social studies. He holds a doctorate in Education from North Carolina State University Raleigh.

About the Authors:

Michael Kabel was English & Language Arts Director for American Book Company. He received his Masters of Fine Arts in Writing from the University of New Orleans and has worked in media, public relations and publishing for fourteen years. His original fiction has appeared in numerous print and online publications, including *JMWW* and *The Baltimore Review*.

Zuzana Urbanek has taught English as a foreign language abroad and in the United States, both to native speakers and as a second language. She holds a Master's degree in English from Arizona State University.

INTRODUCTION TO THE MINNESOTA GRADE 8 READING TEST

The Minnesota Comprehensive Assessment Test in Reading is administered to all Minnesota students enrolled in grade 8 by 2005 – 06 or later. This book offers complete preparation for that test and meets all content standards as described by the Minnesota Department of Education.

In this book, you will prepare for the MCA-II Reading test. First, you will take a pretest to determine your strengths and areas for improvement. In the chapters, you will learn and practice the skills and strategies important to preparing for the test. The last section contains two practice tests that will provide further preparation for the actual test.

FREQUENTLY ASKED QUESTIONS

Will the MCA-II be used to determine promotion for eighth graders?

Successfully completing the MCA-II test is required for all Minnesota eighth graders.

What is tested?

The reading test checks your literary comprehension, understanding of literary devices, knowledge of argument, and information comprehension skills.

When do I take the Minnesota MCA-II Reading Test?

Students will take the MCA-II in late April or early May of their 8th grade year.

How much time do I have to take the exam?

There is no time limit.

When will I get the results?

Schools will notify students of their results at the appropriate time.

Where can I find test information online?

The Web site of the Minnesota Department of Education (www.education.state.mn.us) contains test information.

Test-Taking Quick Tips

1. **Complete the chapters and practice tests in this book.** This text will help you review the skills for the MCA-II Reading Test. The book also contains materials for reviewing skill standards established by the Minnesota Department of Education.

2. **Be prepared.** Get a good night's sleep the day before your exam. Eat a well-balanced meal that contains plenty of proteins and carbohydrates.

3. **Arrive early.** Allow yourself at least 15 – 20 minutes to find your room and get settled before the test starts.

4. **Keep your thoughts positive.** Tell yourself you will do well on the exam.

5. **Practice relaxation techniques.** Talk to a close friend or see a counselor if you stress out before the test. They will suggest ways to deal with anxiety. Some other quick anxiety-relieving exercises include:

    1. **Imagine yourself in your most favorite place.** Sit there and relax.

    2. **Do a body scan.** Tense and relax each part of your body starting with your toes and ending with your forehead.

    3. **Use the 3-12-6 method.** Inhale slowly for 3 seconds. Hold your breath for 12 seconds, then exhale slowly for 6 seconds.

6. **Read directions carefully.** If you don't understand them, ask the proctor for further explanation before the exam starts.

7. **Use your best approach for answering the questions.** Some test-takers like to skim the questions and answers before reading the problem or passage. Others prefer to work the problem or read the passage before looking at the answers. Decide which approach works best for you.

8. **Answer each question on the exam.** Unless you are instructed not to, make sure you answer every question. If you are not sure of an answer, take an educated guess. Eliminate choices that are definitely wrong and then choose from the remaining answers.

9. **Use your answer sheet correctly.** Make sure the number on your question matches the number on your answer sheet. If you need to change your answer, erase it completely. Smudges or stray marks may affect the grading of your exams, particularly if the tests are scored by a computer. If your answers are on a computerized grading sheet, make sure the answers are thoroughly dark. The computerized scanner may skip over answers that are too light.

10. **Check your answers.** Review your exam to make sure you have chosen the best responses. Change answers only if you are absolutely sure they are wrong.

MCA-II Reading Grade 8
Diagnostic Test

The purpose of this diagnostic test is to measure your knowledge in reading comprehension and critical thinking. This diagnostic test is based on the Minnesota standards for English Language Arts and adheres to the sample question format provided by the Minnesota Department of Education.

General Directions:

1. Read all directions carefully.

2. Read each question or sample. Then choose the best answer.

3. Choose only one answer for each question. If you change an answer, be sure to erase your original answer completely.

4. After taking the test, you or your instructor should score it using the evaluation chart following the test. This will enable you to determine your strengths and areas for improvement.

5. You are allowed to take notes in the test book.

Diagnostic Test

Segment 1

> Animals express emotions in surprising ways. Read what researchers are finding. Then answer questions 1 – 8. Some questions may ask you about certain paragraphs. The paragraphs are numbered on the left side of the passage.

Animal Emotions

1   Do elephants cry? Can whales fall in love? Recent evidence suggests that, like humans, animals may experience a variety of emotions ranging from fear and aggression to love, sadness, and joy. In fact, animals and humans also share a similar brain anatomy and chemistry.

2   For many years, scientists believed animals displayed only instincts, such as the impulse to flee from predators or the urge to attack intruders. Scientists called these instincts primary emotions, because they required no conscious thought. Most scientists believed animals were incapable of experiencing higher emotions such as happiness, sadness, or jealousy. One notable exception was the scientist Charles Darwin. He insisted that humans and animals share common emotional links. At that time, few scientists accepted his idea.

3   The basis of early data on animal behavior was experiments using caged animals. Today, scientists frequently watch animals in their natural settings. They conduct field studies which involve careful observations over long periods of time. Researchers take detailed notes on what they see and hear. They photograph and videotape a wide variety of animal behaviors. Then, the scientists complete the scientific process by <u>drawing</u> conclusions based on their observations.

4   As a result of field studies, researchers now know animals display an array of emotions. Elephants do show classic instinctual emotions. They will charge when they sense danger. They will use their massive size and sharp tusks to protect themselves. But, do elephants cry? It appears so. Or at least they mourn, especially when an old elephant dies. The herd stands quietly beside their loved one for days. They form a circle around the remains and touch it with their trunks. They will even form a funeral procession. The herd will carry the bones and tusks of their dead comrade for many miles over many days.

5   A great deal of field research takes place on boats. Whales are the most interesting sea creatures to observe. Based on a recent sighting in the South Atlantic Ocean, scientists believe some whales might be capable of falling in love. The scientists aren't trying to beat around the bush; they want to do more research before making a more definite statement. A researcher observed two whales embracing and rubbing each other with their flippers after they had mated. When they finally swam away, they continued to touch each other.

6   Even dying of a broken heart is possible in the animal world. Primatologist Jane Goodall tells the story of a 50-year-old female chimpanzee who died of old age. Holding her hand and nudging her occasionally, her eight-year-old son refused to leave her lifeless body. Whimpering and moaning, he gradually stopped eating and withdrew from the troop. After mourning more than three weeks, he also died. Goodall concludes that he died of grief.

© Copyright American Book Company. DO NOT DUPLICATE. 1-888-264-5877.

7   Animals show joy and pleasure in their daily lives too. A happy dog wags its tail and jumps for joy at the sight of its master. Cats purr when they're content. After a long absence from each other, even elephants greet their friends by flapping their ears, spinning in circles, and rumbling and roaring in trumpet-like sounds.

8   New research on the brain provides more evidence that humans and animals share similar emotions. Neuroscientists discovered humans and animals share a common brain part called the amygdala. Stimulating this part of the brain creates intense fear. Rats and humans lose their sense of fear after damaging their amygdala. This fact suggests similar wiring in humans and rats.

9   Modern medical research and animal field studies have shown Charles Darwin may have been right all along. Animals, like humans, may be capable of both instinctual and higher levels of emotion.

1. As it is used in paragraph 2, the word <u>drawing</u> means   I.B.3

    A.   lottery.
    B.   sketching.
    C.   process of deciding something.
    D.   pulling or sucking something in.

2. What are primary emotions?   I.C.1

    A.   instincts and impulses
    B.   higher level emotions
    C.   primate-like behavior
    D.   family based emotions

3. What is the main idea of paragraph 4?   I.C.1

    A.   Elephants have tusks and trunks.
    B.   Elephants can stand up for days.
    C.   Researchers have studied elephant herds for days.
    D.   Elephants show sadness when a herd member dies.

4. Which sentence from the passage is an opinion?   I.C.11

    A.   One notable exception was the scientist, Charles Darwin.
    B.   The herd stands quietly beside their loved one for days.
    C.   Whales are the most interesting sea creatures to observe.
    D.   Stimulating this part of the brain creates intense fear.

5. When the author says, "scientists aren't trying to beat around the bush," what does it mean?   I.D.4

    A.   The scientists are avoiding land research.
    B.   The scientists are not evading the issue.
    C.   Whale behavior is difficult to interpret.
    D.   Researchers enjoy studying the whales.

6. Based on the passage, readers can conclude   I.C.4

    A.   field studies are an important part of the study of animal behavior.
    B.   scientists believe all orders of animals have the same brain anatomy.
    C.   elephants have stronger emotions than other animals living in the wild.
    D.   early scientists relied on guessing to form theories on animal behavior.

7. Which sentence shows an elephant is capable of feeling sadness?   I.D.3

    A.   Elephants do show classic instinctual emotions.
    B.   They will charge when they sense danger.
    C.   They will use their massive size and sharp tusks to protect themselves.
    D.   They form a circle around the remains and touch it with their trunks.

Please write the answer to question 8 in your answer book.

8. Summarize the scientific process used in field observations.   I.C.1

> Prior to the end of the Civil War, slaves in the South were not allowed any schooling. Read the following poem about one slave's experience. Then answer questions 9–17. The lines are numbered to help you answer the questions.

Learning to Read
Frances Harper

1 Very soon the Yankee teachers
   Came down and set up school;
But, oh! How the rebs did hate it,—
   It was agin' their rule.

5 Our master always tried to hide
   Book learning from our eyes;
Knowledge didn't agree with slavery—
   'Twould make us all too wise.

9 But some of us would try to steal
   A little from the book,
And put the words together,
   And learn by hook or crook.

13 I remember Uncle Caldwell
   Who took pot liquor fat,
And greased the pages of his book,
   And hid it in his hat.

17 And had his master ever seen
   The leaves upon his head,
He'd have thought them greasy papers,
   But nothing to be read.

21 And there was Mr. Turner's Ben,
   Who heard the children spell,
And picked the words right up by heart,
   And learned to read 'em well.

25 Well, the Northern folks kept sending
   The Yankee teachers down;
And they stood right up and helped us,
   Though Rebs did sneer and frown.

29 And I longed to read my Bible,
   For precious words it said;
But when I began to learn it,
   Folks just shook their heads,

33 And said there is no use trying,
   Oh! Chloe, you're too late;
But as I was rising sixty,
   I had not time to wait.

37 So I got a pair of glasses,
   And straight to work I went,
And never stopped till I could read
   The hymns and Testament.

41 Then I got a little cabin—
   A place to call my own—
And I felt as independent
   As the queen upon her throne.

9. In line 18 of the poem, the word <u>leaves</u> means   I.B.2

    A. depart.
    C. turns over.
    B. foliage.
    D. book pages.

10. What is the main idea of the first two stanzas?   I.C.4

    A. Slave owners did not like Yankees, so the teachers taught slaves instead.

    B. Slave owners did not want slaves attending the Northern teacher's schools.

    C. The Yankees and the Rebs thought slaves were too smart to attend school.

    D. The slaves tried to hide whenever the Yankee teachers came into town.

11. The reader can conclude that the speaker most likely believed   I.C.4

    A. no one wanted to help slaves.

    B. you are never too old to learn.

    C. the slave owners knew what was best.

    D. books were not worthy of proper care.

12. Which statement best reflects the theme of the poem?   I.C.4

    A. Never give up.

    B. Easy come, easy go.

    C. A woman's home is her castle.

    D. Jack of all trades, master of none.

13. Which line shows the speaker's motivation for learning to read?   I.D.3

    A. And I longed to read my Bible,

    B. I remember Uncle Caldwell,

    C. And learned to read 'em well

    D. Then I got a little cabin—

14. The author wrote this poem most likely to   I.D.3

    A. describe how slaves hid reading material.

    B. compare teachers in the North and South.

    C. show the challenges slaves overcame to learn how to read.

    D. explain the difference between older and younger learners.

15. Which line from the poem is a simile?   I.D7:

    A. 'Twould make us all too wise.

    B. And learn by hook or crook.

    C. And straight to work I went,

    D. As the queen upon her throne.

16. Which is the best summary of lines 33 through 40?   I.C.1

    A. No one thought Chloe could learn how to read.

    B. Chloe wore a pair of eyeglasses to help her read.

    C. Despite discouragement from others, Chloe worked to meet her goal.

    D. Chloe was too old to learn how to read the Testaments and Hymns.

17. By telling the poem from Chloe's point of view, the author helps the reader better understand   I.C.14

    A. Chloe's determination to learn how to read.

    B. the slave owner's concerns about the schools.

    C. Ben's excitement over learning how to spell.

    D. the Yankee teachers' desire to open schools.

Segment 2

> Two writers express their views on genetic engineering. Read the following letters to the editor. Then answer questions 18–25. Some questions require you to reread certain paragraphs. Paragraphs are numbered for reference.

Letters to the Editor [Cloning]

Dear Editor:

1 I am writing in regard to your recent article on genetic engineering. I believe you presented a <u>lopsided</u> view of the issue by omitting key points. Since the middle of the twentieth century, genetic engineering has impacted society. Scientists apply the process, which changes the genetic makeup of plants and animals, to agriculture and medical research.

2 Scientists use genetic engineering to modify plants. The modified plants are stronger than naturally grown plants. They produce more fruits, grains, and vegetables. The result is an increase in world food production to help support the growing population.

3 Cloning is only one aspect of genetic engineering. Cloning uses a cell from one organism to create a second organism. The second organism is identical to the original. Over the last decade, cloning, especially the prospect of reproductive human cloning, has gained worldwide attention.

4 Scientists have cloned many different animals. The first known clone was a tadpole. The cloning took place in 1952. Forty-five years later, the world heard about a sheep named Dolly. Born in Scotland, Dolly was the first mammal ever created by cloning. Her creation sparked worldwide interest and concern. Your article used that concern and fed into the belief that tomorrow we will be creating our own twins.

5 There is still much to be learned about cloning and no thinking person would deny the ethical questions involved in the issue. However, data learned from cloning could lead to the development of healthier livestock. Cell cloning also has a major impact on medical research. Scientists use the process to develop new medicines. Research in cloning may lead to cures for life altering diseases like diabetes and Alzheimer's disease.

6 I hope in the future, your paper will strive to present both sides of the issue.

Mary E. Cooper

Dear Editor:

7   I am writing in response to Mary Cooper's letter regarding your article on genetic engineering.

8   Ms. Cooper wrote about the positive impact of modifying plant life. However, she failed to cite the negative impact it has on poor farmers. The special fertilizers and pesticides used on modified plants make this type of plant too costly for many farmers to grow. If the financial stress it is causing farmers isn't enough to cause Ms. Cooper to think again, the health effects of these chemicals on both farmers and consumers should be cause to reevaluate her judgment.

9   As far as the cloning process is concerned, Ms. Cooper should consider the lack of balance found in her letter. I agree cloning lacks sufficient research, and the issue opens many ethical questions. However, Ms. Cooper seems to be advocating going forth blindly without first finding solutions to these issues.

10   The facts she failed to include show cloning is inefficient and has produced a large proportion of unhealthy offspring. More than 90 percent of cloning attempts result in failure. Those clones that survive to birth have a high chance of dying early in life and experience very high rates of birth defects. The animals show increased tumor growth and disease. Dolly survived only to the age of six, though her life expectancy was 11 to 12 years.

11   Cloning and genetic engineering are issues that go to the core of our value systems. Individuality, family, and religious values are factors that can't be ignored.

Kevin M. Rogers

18. What is the main idea of Mary E. Cooper's letter?   I.C.1

    A. The world population is increasing.

    B. Scientists know how to modify plants.

    C. The world needs more produce to feed the growing population.

    D. Genetic engineering and cloning have positive effects on society.

19. Which detail sentence would best support the main idea in paragraph 3?   I.C.1

    A. The sole purpose of genetic engineering is cloning.

    B. Computer technology has also advanced medical research.

    C. This attention has caused many people to lose sight of the bigger picture.

    D. Many consumers still prefer to purchase produce grown without chemicals.

20. Based on Ms. Cooper's letter, reader can infer that Dolly's creation caused concern over   I.C.4

    A. the possibility of human cloning.

    B. the gap in research between countries.

    C. the time span between the tadpole and sheep cloning.

    D. the financial investment in genetic engineering research.

21. In Ms. Cooper's letter, the word lop-sided means   I.B.2

    A. entertaining.

    B. informative.

    C. evenhanded.

    D. unbalanced.

22. Read the following sentence from Kevin Rogers' letter.   I.C.14

> Those clones that survive to birth have a high chance of dying early in life and experience very high rates of birth defects.

Mr. Rogers included this information to show

- **A.** more experimentation is needed.
- **B.** the cloning process is very risky.
- **C.** sheep are not good subjects for cloning.
- **D.** cloning has no scientific documentation.

23. Which is the best summary of Mr. Rogers' letter?   I.C.1

- **A.** The positive effects of genetic engineering should also be considered.
- **B.** Ms. Cooper shows a lack of respect for the values and ethics of society.
- **C.** Both modifying plant life and cloning have negative effects on society.
- **D.** Plant modification has been successful, but cloning has mainly failed.

24. What idea is found in both Ms. Cooper's letter and Mr. Rogers' letter?   I.C.11

- **A.** The cloning of Dolly was successful.
- **B.** Cloning involves many ethical issues.
- **C.** The quality of life for farmers increased with the creation of modified plants.
- **D.** The results of genetic engineering research have received very little publicity.

Please write the answer to question 25 in your answer book.

25. Compare Ms. Cooper's and Mr. Rogers' points of view on genetically modified plants. Include two details to support each point of view.   I.D.12

Segment 3

Some state and local laws can still be enforced even though they are outdated. Read about these laws. Then answer questions 26–33. Some questions may ask you about certain paragraphs. The paragraphs are numbered on the left side of the passage.

Is That Legal?

1   Are you planning a cross country trip? If so, before packing the car brush up on the laws in the places you plan to visit. Some state and local laws are terribly outdated, but authorities failed to repeal them. Learn about these obscure laws, and avoid getting tangled in the legal system as you travel the open road.

2   Some of the laws reflect the safety concerns of days gone by. For example, putting salt on a railroad track in Alabama is a crime punishable by death. Other laws make you wonder what kinds of things were dangerous long ago. For example, it is illegal in Wichita, Kansas, to carry a concealed bean snapper. Were people roaming Wichita stealing string beans from unsuspecting farmers? Can a bean snapper be a weapon? The answer is a mystery but when traveling in Wichita, make sure your bean snapper is visible to all passersby.

3   While traveling through Kansas with your bean snapper exposed, be aware of another old law still on the books. You cannot have a mule on a Kansas road in August, unless the mule wears a straw hat. If it happens to be Sunday and you stop walking your mule for a bite to eat, think carefully about your order. Officials enacted a law there making it illegal for restaurants in Kansas to serve cherry pie *a la mode* on Sundays.

4   If you are ready to pack up your bean snapper and move on, consider this law before choosing your next destination. In Youngstown, Ohio, it is illegal to run out of gas. If that law deterred you, then you may want to sleep on this one before visiting Pennsylvania. In Pennsylvania, when a team of horses comes toward you, you must pull off the road and cover the vehicle with a blanket in order to let the horses pass. If the timid horses won't pass, you must take apart the vehicle, piece by piece, and hide it under the bushes.

5   Before tossing your suitcase in the trunk, double check and make sure you have packed appropriately. Numerous states have laws about attire. You can't wear a hat while dancing in Fargo, North Dakota. In Chicago, fishing in your pajamas is a crime. Gentlemen, if your travel plans include Carmel, New York, remember, a man cannot go outside unless his clothes match.

6   Ladies, don't chuckle too quickly. In Tucson, Arizona, officials outlawed women wearing pants in public. St. Croix, Wisconsin doesn't ban any particular type of clothing. However, no woman may wear anything red in public. That is the silliest law still on the books. That law will seem lax if your next stop is Charlotte, North Carolina. You might want to limit yourself to winter visits to that city. Women in this city must cover themselves in at least 16 yards of cloth at all times.

7   Some states see flaws in their laws and amend them. In Kentucky, women may wear a bathing suit beside a highway. However, if not armed with a club or accompanied by at least two police escorts, the women face arrest. Some wise officials saw flaws in this law. They amended it to specify that it applied only to women weighing between 90 and 200 pounds, who were not female horses.

8   Your behavior is also subject to many city and state laws. Never flirt on the street in Little Rock, Arkansas. It is punishable by 30 days in jail. If you are trying to avoid jail time, never make an ugly face at a dog in Oklahoma, or tease a skunk in Minnesota. No matter how tempted you might be, never, never, never catch a fish with a lasso in Tennessee.

9   Will someone really arrest you for falling asleep in a cheese factory in South Dakota? Probably not, but it is fun to read about the obscure laws across the country. It is even more fun imagining why these laws ever existed.

26. Read the dictionary entry below.

> obscure-*adj* (1) dark or dim; (2) faint; (3) relatively unknown; (4) secluded

Which is the meaning of the word **obscure** in paragraphs 1 and 9?

A.   dark or dim
B.   faint
C.   relatively unknown
D.   secluded

27. The speaker assumes readers will travel cross country by

A.   car.
B.   mule.
C.   foot.
D.   train.

28. The speaker suggests women visit Charlotte, North Carolina in the winter because

A.   skiing is legal in North Carolina.
B.   they should visit Arizona first.
C.   the laws are not enforced in the winter.
D.   summer is too hot to wear that much fabric.

29. In paragraph 4, why most likely would the horses be frightened?

A.   The horses were also subject to numerous unusual laws.
B.   Automobiles were uncommon when the law was enacted.
C.   Horses raised in Pennsylvania are more easily frightened.
D.   The speed limit for vehicles in Pennsylvania is very high.

30. Which sentence from the passage is an opinion?

A.   That is the silliest law still on the books.
B.   Never flirt on the street in Little Rock, Arkansas.
C.   Some states see flaws in their laws and amend them.
D.   Your behavior is also subject to many city and state laws.

31. In paragraph 4, when the speaker says, "you may want to sleep on this one," what does the speaker mean?   I.D.4

   A. It is legal to sleep in your car in Pennsylvania.

   B. You will need a nap after taking apart your vehicle.

   C. Take a day to think it over before making a decision.

   D. Make sure you sleep on the long journey from Kansas.

32. Which of the following statements best reflects the theme of this passage?   I.D.12

   A. It's a small world.

   B. Always be prepared.

   C. A rose is a rose by any other name.

   D. A penny saved is a penny earned.

33. The author most likely wrote this passage to   I.D.12

   A. entertain readers with amusing facts.

   B. explain the reasoning behind the laws.

   C. persuade lawmakers to repeal the laws.

   D. compare state and local legal systems.

What is geothermal energy? How is it being used? Read about this energy resource. Then answer questions 34 – 40. Some of the questions will require you to refer to the numbered paragraphs.

Geothermal Energy

1   Geothermal energy refers to the heat energy deep inside the earth. Tapping into this natural resource can provide warmth and power without polluting the environment. The heat from the earth's core continuously flows outward. When temperatures and pressures become high enough, some mantle rock melts, becoming magma. The magma moves slowly toward Earth's crust carrying the heat from below. Most often, the magma remains below Earth's crust. It heats rainwater that seeped deep into the earth and nearby rock. Sometimes the rock and water gets as hot as 700° F. Some of this hot geothermal water reaches the earth's surface as hot springs or geysers, but most of it stays deep underground. Scientists call this collection of hot water a geothermal reservoir.

2   Engineers drill wells into the reservoirs and bring the hot water to the surface. Once at the surface, the water and steam help generate electricity in geothermal power plants. Steam, heat, or hot water from reservoirs provides the force that spins the turbine generators and produces electricity. The used geothermal water is recycled. It travels down an injection well into the reservoir. The reheated water then returns to the plant and generates more electricity. This process helps maintain pressure and sustain the reservoir.

3   What is the environmental impact of geothermal energy? The impact is a positive one. The greatest advantage is that it is so clean. Geothermal power plants do not burn fossil fuels. Generating electricity with hot, underground water helps conserve non-renewable fossil fuels. By decreasing the use of these fuels, we reduce air pollution. There is no smoky air around geothermal power plants. In fact, engineers build these power plants in the middle of farm crops and forests. They are safe enough to share land with cattle and local wildlife. For ten years, Lake County, California has been home to five geothermal electric power plants. It is the first and only county in California to meet the strictest air quality standards in the U.S.

4   The land area required for geothermal power plants is smaller per megawatt than for almost every other type of power plant. Geothermal plants do not require the damming of rivers or harvesting of forests. There are no mine shafts, tunnels, open pits, waste heaps, or oil spills. Other energy sources <u>feed</u> into these problems. These power plants run economically. They run 24 hours a day, all year. The plant sits right on top of its fuel source. Neither weather nor wars disrupt service because this energy form requires no transportation. Transportation problems greatly affect other fuel sources.

Geothermal Well in Zunil, Guatemala

5   The use of geothermal energy for electricity has grown worldwide. It now provides about 7,000 megawatts in 21 countries. The United States alone produces 2700 megawatts of electricity from geothermal energy. This is comparable to transporting and burning 60 million barrels of oil each year.

6   One method of using geothermal energy is the Geothermal Heat Pump (GHP). About 6 feet below the surface in your back yard, the temperature is about 45–58°. A GHP can circulate water through pipes in your back yard to the walls in your house. It will cool your house in the summer and heat it in the winter. In the winter, since the underground temperature would still be about 50 degrees or so, you would still need a gas furnace or electric heat to supplement the GHP. The pumps require very little electricity and are easy on the environment. Because they don't require the drilling depth or geothermal power plants, they are relatively inexpensive to use. In the United States, over 500,000 homes, schools, and other buildings use GHPs to heat and cool their buildings.

7   In Klamath Falls, Oregon, GHP pipes run under the roads and sidewalks. This keeps the ice thawed in the winter. In New Mexico, where the growing season is short, the pipes run through farmlands among vegetable plants.

8   All citizens who care about the environment favor geothermal energy. Its environment friendly process makes it the energy of the future.

34. Read the following sentences from paragraph 3 of the passage.   I.C.6

> For ten years, Lake County, California has been home to five geothermal electric power plants. It is the first and only county in California to meet the strictest air quality standards in the U.S.

The author includes this information as evidence that geothermal power plants

    A. work best in warm areas.

    B. are not a new technology.

    C. were first built in the U.S.

    D. do not cause air pollution.

35. Based on the passage, which most likely is a disadvantage of geothermal power plants?   I.C.4

    A. They destroy earth's natural resources.

    B. It is very expensive to drill into the earth.

    C. They use up the energy found inside the earth.

    D. Plants can only be constructed in lowland regions.

36. As it is used in paragraph 4, the word <u>feed</u> means   I.B.3

    A. furnish or supply.

    B. food for livestock.

    C. to supply a signal to an electronic circuit.

    D. passing a ball or puck to a team member.

37. The author, most likely, wrote this passage to   I.D.12

    A. explain how readers can build a geothermal power plant.

    B. persuade readers to increase their use of geothermal energy.

    C. compare the positive and negative effects of geothermal energy.

    D. show the environmental concerns that affect countries worldwide.

38. In New Mexico, GHP is used on farms to   I.C.4

    A. water the crops.

    B. light the fields.

    C. extend the growing season.

    D. increase available acreage.

39. The author most likely wrote this passage for   I.C.14

    A. energy experts.

    B. energy consumers.

    C. geothermal engineers.

    D. oil company executives.

Please write the answer to question 40 in your answer book.

40. Summarize how geothermal energy is produced.   I.C.1

Movies, books, and dramas about vampires are popular in today's culture. Read about the realities behind the vampire myths. Then answer questions 41 – 48. Some questions refer to certain paragraphs. The paragraphs are numbered on the left side of the passage.

The Vampire or the Vampire Bat?

1   Was the vampire bat named for the mythical vampires, or was the mythical vampire named for the bat? How are the creatures alike? How are they different?

2   There are countless tales and legends of the mythical creatures called vampires. The origins of the vampire legend are ancient with some myths dating back to the 4th century. The legends arose in many cultures. What most stories have in common is that vampires were once living people, but are now "the walking dead." These mythical creatures stalk the living and drink their blood. In most myths, vampires are evil demon-like beings.

3   Modern Western ideas about vampires come mainly from Bram Stoker's novel, *Dracula*. The novel, written in 1897, is still popular today. In creating his main character of Count Dracula, Stoker invented a new type of vampire. This vampire had more human characteristics and participated in society. Count Dracula's name came from a real-life historical figure, Vlad Dracul. Dracul was reportedly a cruel and brutal Romanian prince. Some people speculate Vlad Dracul may have had a rare disease sometimes mistaken for vampirism, and perhaps this is what interested Stoker. But the author probably just liked his name, which means dragon or devil, and the mystery surrounding the man.

4   Whatever his inspiration, Stoker created an original vampire, which became the basis of many others. Most importantly, Stoker forever linked the vampire bat to the vampire legend. In the book, Dracula often takes the form of a bat. About a century before Dracula's publication, a species of bats called vampire bats was discovered in Latin America. This species of bats did not exist in Eastern Europe, the setting for Dracula. Yet, somehow Stoker made the connection.

5   The vampire bat is only about two or three inches long with a wingspan of eight inches. It's a cute little creature that you are sure to love. Like its literary counterpart, the vampire bat has sharp teeth that pierce the skin of its sleeping victims. Unlike mythical vampires, vampire bats do not suck their victim's blood. Instead, they <u>lap</u> up the flowing blood with their tongues.

6   Vampire bats don't stalk their dinner. They use echolocation to find their prey. The bats emit sound waves and wait for them to reflect off their victims. Then, they depend on the heat sensors on their noses to select the perfect spot to sink their teeth. These bats drink the blood of cows, pigs, horses, and other livestock. Like the mythical vampires, vampire bats will dine on human blood.

7   The livestock and people bitten by bats do not die from blood loss. However, bats can spread rabies. Rabies is the basis for one theory behind the bats and vampire connection. Rabies affects the central nervous system. In Stoker's time, the disease was fatal. Today, a vaccine can save victims from that fate. When some livestock contracted rabies from vampire bat bites, the farmers thought it was vampirism. Although most bats do not carry the disease, people link the flying mammal's blood drinking ways with rabies, and thus with mythical vampires.

41. As it is used in paragraph 5, the word lap means   I.B.3

   A.   a polishing tool.

   B.   to hold protectively.

   C.   the distance covered on a track.

   D.   to take in drink with the tongue.

42. What is the main idea of paragraph 2?   I.C.1

   A.   Many things inspired Bram Stoker.

   B.   Vampire bats lived in Latin America.

   C.   Stoker linked the vampire bat with the vampire myth.

   D.   Vampire bats were not discovered in Eastern Europe.

43. Which statement from the passage is an opinion?   I.C.11

   A.   The legends arose in many cultures.

   B.   Vampire bats don't stalk their dinner.

   C.   In the book, Dracula often takes the form of a bat.

   D.   It's a cute little creature that you are sure to love.

44. Bram Stoker, most likely, chose Dracula for his vampire's name because   I.C.1

   A.   he was fascinated by Vlad Dracul.

   B.   it was a common term used for bats.

   C.   dracula is the Romanian word for vampire.

   D.   it was often used in Eastern European legends.

45. In paragraph 6, the word prey means   I.B.2

   A.   sound waves.

   B.   heat sensors.

   C.   an animal taken by a predator as food.

   D.   homes shared with mythical vampires.

46. Why, most likely, was rabies a fatal disease in Stoker's time?   I.C.4

   A.   There was no vaccination available.

   B.   There were more bats in the area.

   C.   People did not seek medical help.

   D.   Rabies mainly affected the elderly.

47. The reader can conclude the author believes   I.C.4

   A.   a vampire bat's bite can cause vampirism.

   B.   vampire bat bites do not cause real damage.

   C.   early vampire myths were based on historical truths.

   D.   Bram Stoker's *Dracula* is deservedly a literary classic.

48. Which organizational method does the author use to present the information?   I.D.12

   A.   chronological

   B.   space order

   C.   compare/contrast

   D.   cause and effect

GRADE 8 MCA-II TEST DIAGNOSTIC EXAM IN READING

EVALUATION CHART

Directions: On the following chart, circle the question numbers that you answered incorrectly and evaluate the results. Then turn to the appropriate topics (organized by chapters), read the explanations, and complete the exercises. Review other chapters as necessary. Finally, complete the **two practice tests** to further prepare yourself for the Minnesota Grade 8 MCA-II test.

Chapter	Page Number	Content Standards	Questions
Chapter 1: Word Meaning		I.B.2, I.B.3	1, 9, 21, 26, 36, 41, 45
Chapter 2: Details, Main Ideas, Summarizing		I.C.1	2, 3, 8, 16, 18, 19, 23, 40, 42, 44
Chapter 3: Drawing Conclusions, Making Inferences		I.C.4	6, 10, 12, 20, 27, 28, 35, 3?, 46, 47
Chapter 4: Fact and Opinion		I.C.11	4, 24, 43
Chapter 5: Evaluating Author's Evidence		I.C.6, I.C.14	17, 22, 34, 39
Chapter 6: Author's Purpose		I.C.14	17, 22, 25, 32, 33, 37, 39, 48
Chapter 7: Characters in Literature		I.D.3	7, 3, 14
Chapter 8: Figurative Language in Poetry and Prose		I.D.4, I.D.7	11, 15, 31
Chapter 9: Writing the Constructed Response		I.C.1, I.C.4, I.C.6, I.C.1?, I.D.3, I.D?, I.D.7, I.D.12	8, 25, 40
Chapter 10: Comparing and Contrasting		I.D.12	25, 48

Chapter 1
Word Meaning

This chapter covers Minnesota Reading Standard(s):

| I.B.2 and I.B.3 | Students will determine the meaning of unknown words by using a dictionary or context clues. |
| | Students will recognize and interpret words with multiple meanings. |

As children, we all begin speaking with simple words such as cup, toy, and dog. This is the beginning of spoken vocabulary. Similarly, as we read we learn simple words first, often by sight. Then we learn to sound out the syllables of longer words. As readers, we improve our level of reading by continuously building on our vocabulary. The process of adding to your vocabulary and discovering new words can be accomplished by building on **root words** with **prefixes** and **suffixes**, developing better **dictionary skills**, and interpreting words with **multiple meanings** using **context clues**. These tools are part of the building blocks that you will need to develop a deeper understanding of what you read.

Learning new words is an important process that often takes some analysis. To **analyze** means to look closely at something to gain an understanding of its small units or parts. Words are often made up of smaller parts that act as clues to the whole word's meaning. Part of analyzing words is studying their **derivation**: how words are formed from smaller parts consisting of **prefixes**, **suffixes**, and **root words**.

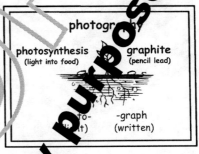

The **dictionary** and the **thesaurus** are resources we have for investigating word meaning. The dictionary provides a listing of words, their meanings, their pronunciations, and their uses. A good dictionary includes more than just correct spelling. In fact, it may include the origin of words, a sample sentence, and part of speech. The thesaurus contains **synonyms** (similar words) and **antonyms** (opposite words). Using one is an excellent way to develop your ability to use unfamiliar words.

Being a naturally good speller is rare because spelling in the English language is not always logical. Because of this, the spelling of many words in English is best memorized. Learn your own strengths and weaknesses in spelling and use the methods taught in this chapter that best help you become a stronger speller.

WORD DERIVATIONS AND ANALYSIS

Since many words are made up of smaller parts, breaking them down into their smallest units is one way to determine word meaning. Different words can be formed or derived from one root word. This is called **derivation**. Root words originate mostly from Latin or Greek, which were two of the first influences on the English language. **Word analysis** includes the process of determining the meaning of words based on the meanings of their smaller parts called **roots** (the main parts of a word), **prefixes** (the beginnings of words), and **suffixes** (the endings of words).

For example, in the word **extraterrestrial**, "extra" is a prefix (one or more letters or syllables added to the beginning of a word) that means outside or beyond. The root "terra" comes from the Latin word for earth. The letters "ial" at the end of a word form a suffix which means act of, like, ours. By dividing extraterrestrial into its smallest units, you discover that it means "as beyond the earth."

Space Shuttle *Discovery*
Docking at the International Space Station

You can use the same process for other words. The root "dor" found in **dormant** and **dormitory** comes from the Latin word for sleep. Dormant means inactive, as in sleep, and dormitory refers to a building with sleeping quarters.

Learning the word parts in the lists below will unlock the meanings of countless words in your reading. Mark the ones you do not know, and then learn their meanings.

Prefixes					
Prefix	Meaning	Example	Prefix	Meaning	Example
ab	from	absurd	in	not	inept
ad	to	advocate	inter	between	interstate
anti	against	antibody	intra	within	intranet
be	thoroughly	befuddle	mis	bad, wrong	misread
com, con	with	community	post	after	postgraduate
de	reverse	decompose	pre	before	preheat
dis	not	disinterested	pro	onward	progress
en	the state of	entangle	re	back again	recapture
ex	out	exit	sub	under	subspecies
il	not	illegal	un	not	untold

Roots

Root	Meaning	Example	Root	Meaning	Example
ann	year	annual	mult	many	multifaceted
aqua	water	aquamarine	path	feeling	telepathy
aud	hear	audible	phon	sound	phonics
bio	life	biology	port	carry	portfolio
cent	hundred	century	rad	ray	radar
chron	time	chronicle	scope	see	telescope
dic	to speak	dictate	scrib	to write	scripture
fort	strong	fortress	tele	distance	telegraph
gen	race, kind	genesis	trib	give, assign	tribute
gratis	pleasing	grateful	varius	changing, many	variety
ject	throw	interject			
med	middle	mediator	ven	to come, go	convention
			viv, vit	life	vivacious

Suffixes

Suffix	Meaning	Examples	Suffix	Meaning	Examples
able	capable of being	capable, unbeatable	ly	in like manner	confidently, boisterously
age	related to	marriage, foliage	less	without	meaningless, thoughtless
al, ial	act of like	special, genial	logy	study of	biology, theology
ance	state or quality of	furtherance, performance	ment	condition of	contentment, entanglement
er, or	one who	buyer, actor	ness	quality, condition	kindness, likeness
ful	full of	wonderful, bountiful	ous	full of	clamorous, poisonous
hood	state of	fatherhood parenthood	ship	position held	kinship chairmanship
ish	having the quality of	clannish, sluggish	tion	action, or state of being	motion, education
itis	inflammation	bronchitis, gingivitis	ure	process of	overture, adventure
ive	having the nature of	positive, progressive	ward	in a specified direction	onward, afterward

Practice 1: Writing with Roots

People often have trouble budgeting their time successfully in order to meet deadlines. In a paragraph of advice to younger students, tell about a situation in which you had trouble managing your time. Explain how you resolved this problem. Include five root words from the previous page along with prefixes or suffixes, and underline them.

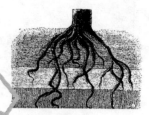

Practice 2: Word Derivation and Analysis

On your own paper, divide each of the following words into prefixes, suffixes, and roots (when possible), and explain how these parts make up the meaning of the word. If you need help, consult a dictionary.

Example: illegible

il (not) + leg(ere) (to read) + ible (capable of being) = not capable of being read

1. inscribe	5. supplement	9. restore
2. sugar	6. hullabaloo	10. extraneous
3. bronchitis	7. bilingual	11. prediction
4. misadvise	8. introvert	12. pathology

Practice 3: Word Analysis

Match the prefix, suffix, or root with its meaning.

Matching Prefixes

_____ 1. sub	A.	reverse
_____ 2. ad	B.	again
_____ 3. in	C.	out
_____ 4. com	D.	under
_____ 5. ex	E.	thoroughly
_____ 6. pro	F.	not
_____ 7. ab	G.	to
_____ 8. pre	H.	with
_____ 9. be	I.	onward
_____ 10. re	J.	before
_____ 11. en	K.	from
_____ 12. de	L.	state of

Matching Roots

_____ 13. ject	A.	year
_____ 14. chron	B.	k
_____ 15. scrib	C.	
_____ 16. gen	D.	feeling
_____ 17. tele		write
_____ 18. ann	F.	come
_____ 19. port	G.	throw
_____ 20. rad	H.	sound
_____ 21. path	I.	hear
_____ 22.	J.	distance
_____ 23. aud	K.	time
_____ 24. phon	L.	to carry

Matching Suffixes

_____ 25. logy	_____ 31. age	A. inflammation	G. in a direction
_____ 26. itis	_____ 32. tion	B. capable of	H. state of being
_____ 27. ment	_____ 33. ship	C. one who	I. full of
_____ 28. ward	_____ 34. ful	D. related to	J. position held
_____ 29. ly	_____ 35. er	E. study of	K. without
_____ 30. less	_____ 36. able	F. condition of	L. in like manner

Practice 4: Word Analysis Passage

Read the following article for content and then answer the questions after it.

Pilgrim Life

When the Pilgrims landed in November of 1620 on the shore of what is now called Massachusetts, they needed to find food and build shelter if they were to survive. There were no stores or **markets** for buying supplies, and no houses for the Pilgrims to move into. All the needs had to be met by themselves, and even the smallest hands **contributed** to that effort. A **hearty** group though, the Pilgrims proved able to overcome their **dire** predicament and many **hardships** to establish an enduring colony which they named Plymouth.

The first winter was brutal and cold. Many of those who crossed the ocean to **attain** freedom never saw the next spring. Those who did survive focused on making preparations for spring planting. Their hard work that first year was rewarded with a **copious** harvest in the autumn of 1621, and the Pilgrims celebrated the first Thanksgiving as a time of **gratitude**.

One of the **precepts** that the Pilgrims lived by was that hard work is one of life's greatest virtues. They believed that settling the wilderness of the New World was their **destiny**, so they were driven to survive despite the **bleakest** of circumstances. After that first Thanksgiving celebration, the Pilgrims realized that their **perceived** destiny might come true.

Indeed it did! Over the next several years, Plymouth grew into a successful community of 180 colonists. By 1627, more than one-third of them were age sixteen or younger. There were no schools, but after working hard in the fields during the day the children enjoyed reading at home at night. Their work centered on providing **sustenance** for the family. The children's chores **varied**, depending on their age and abilities, but by the time they were six, most were working a full day alongside their parents. These hard-working children became hard-working adults who passed on their determination and sense of destiny to their own

Word Meaning

children. This pattern continued for generations as a new nation emerged to become one of the most **fortitudinal** nations in history.

Take a moment to study the words (focus on their prefixes, roots, and suffixes) that are bolded and underlined in the passage. Then, for each of the following words from the passage, choose the response that is closest in meaning to the word's use in the passage. In some cases, you may need to consult a dictionary.

1. **markets:**
   A. stocks
   B. cities
   C. stores
   D. customers

2. **contributed:**
   A. added to
   B. checked on
   C. worked against
   D. took away from

3. **hearty:**
   A. smart
   B. inventive
   C. weak
   D. strong

4. **dire:**
   A. understood
   B. special
   C. serious
   D. scary

5. **hardships:**
   A. wooden boats
   B. difficulties
   C. crimes
   D. circumstances

6. **attain:**
   A. regain
   B. refrain
   C. detain
   D. obtain

7. **copious:**
   A. tasty
   B. well-deserved
   C. plentiful
   D. special

8. **gratitude:**
   A. thankfulness
   B. gracefulness
   C. charity
   D. mercilessness

9. **precepts:**
   A. behaviors
   B. oddities
   C. blessings
   D. beliefs

10. **destiny:**
    A. past course
    B. future course
    C. present course
    D. main course

11. **bleakest:**
    A. most desperate
    B. weakest
    C. coldest
    D. most challenging

12. **perceived:**
    A. misunderstood
    B. understood
    C. learned
    D. unlearned

13. **sustenance:**
    A. security
    B. suffering
    C. food
    D. substance

22

14. <u>varied</u>:

    A. became more difficult   B. became easier   C. became more challenging   D. became different

15. <u>fortitudinal</u>:

    A. strong   B. fort building   C. weakest   D. giving

DICTIONARY SKILLS AND MULTIPLE MEANINGS

There are many types of dictionaries, and each contains a surprising amount of information, including much more than just correct spelling. There are **abridged**, or "abbreviated," dictionaries and **unabridged** dictionaries. Unabridged dictionaries will have some or all of the following features for each entry word:

1. An entry which shows the correct spelling (Example: magnify)

2. The pronunciation shown by syllabication, accent marks, and sometimes a re-spelling (mag′ ne fi)

3. The part of speech label (such as *n* for "noun," *v* for "verb," and *adj.* for "adjective")

4. The etymology, or origin, of the word (magni - Latin)

5. The meaning(s) of the word (magnify). Multiple meanings are:

    a. to increase the apparent size of, as a lens does

    b. to make greater in actual size; enlarge

    c. to cause to seem greater or more important; attribute too much importance to; exaggerate

    d. to make more exciting; intensify; dramatize; heighten

    e. to extol; praise

6. Examples of the word in context (Deborah used a microscope to *magnify* the bacteria.)

7. Special usage labels which identify words that are used in unusual ways

8. Related word forms

9. Synonyms (similar *enlarge*), antonyms (opposite *shrink*), and sometimes idioms (figures of speech)

Most **dictionary** entries have more than one definition. Some words have multiple meanings. When you look up a word, you must decide which definition is most appropriate for the context in which the word is used. To do so, use the strategies on the following page.

STRATEGIES FOR LEARNING DEFINITIONS AND MULTIPLE MEANINGS

1. *Read all of the definitions of a dictionary entry.* Suppose that the italicized word in the following sample sentence is unfamiliar to you. You would look up *course* in the dictionary, and read the following multiple definitions.

   The *course* the captain chose would take the ship dangerously close to the icebergs.

   course \ kōrs \ **A** *n* (13c) **1.** The act or action of moving in a path from point to point **2.** Accustomed procedure or normal action [the law taking its **course**] **3.** An ordered process or succession **4.** A part of a meal served at one time. **B** *v* **1.** to follow close upon **2.** To hunt or pursue with hounds **3.** run or move swiftly through.

2. *If the word can be more than one part of speech, decide which part of speech the word is in the sentence.* Then concentrate on the definitions for that part of speech. In a dictionary entry, the part-of-speech label is italicized and comes before the definitions. In the sentence above, *course* is a noun and the subject of the sentence. Of the noun definitions in the entry, only one is appropriate.

3. *Read the sentence to yourself, substituting each correct part-of-speech definition for the word. Decide which one best fits the sentence.* The appropriate definition for *course*, as it is used in the sentence, is the second:

   The *act or action of moving in a path from point to point* the captain chose would take the ship dangerously close to the icebergs.

4. *If there is more than one entry for a word, read each entry completely.* Some words are homographs: they are spelled alike but have different origins and meanings. For example, the words *board* meaning "a piece of wood" and *board* meaning "to get on to" are homographs. Homographs are given separate entries in the dictionary. Be sure to choose the correct meaning for your sentence.

For a short list of homographs, see the chart below. In the dictionary, locate two meanings and two parts of speech. Then write each one in a sentence.

Some Common Homographs			
abandon	domino	novelty	shade
bound	flavor	produce	lift
conserve	minor	retreat	trump

Practice 5: Finding Appropriate Definitions

Using a dictionary, find the appropriate definition of the italicized word in each of the following sentences. *Step 1:* Write the appropriate dictionary definition. *Step 2:* Write a sentence of your own, using the word with this definition.

1. Because Dylan's *conduct* was satisfactory, he was allowed to lead during the field trip.

   Definition _____

   Sentence _____

2. The Secret Service *escorted* the president to the luncheon at the capitol.

   Definition _____

   Sentence _____

3. The aircraft carrier was accompanied by six destroyer *escorts*.

   Definition _____

   Sentence _____

4. Last summer, my family and I were finally able to go on vacation to a *resort* in the Rocky Mountains.

   Definition _____

   Sentence _____

5. The orchestra director *conducted* the most beautiful performance of Handel's <u>Messiah</u>.

   Definition _____

   Sentence _____

6. The workers from J.P.'s Glassworks Company removed a panel from the door of the new house and *glazed* it.

   Definition _____

   Sentence _____

7. In a moment of desperation, the driver *resorted* to swerving into the ditch to avoid hitting the out-of-control motorcycle.

   Definition _____

   Sentence _____

Practice 6: Discovering Correct Definitions

Each italicized word in the passage below has a number after it. After you read the passage, look up the word in a dictionary and find the appropriate definition for the sentence. Then write out these definitions on a separate piece of paper.

Cappuccino

This is a caffeine consumer's guide to *ostentatious* **(1)** coffee *concoctions* **(2)** for those people who want a break from *domestic* **(3)** coffees. Read on and be prepared to *saunter* **(4)** into the local chain store selling overpriced, over-commercialized brew. If your taste buds are happiest when *assailed* **(5)** with sharp, bitter sensations, then espresso is for you. Espresso is created when scalding hot tap water is forced through *robust* **(6)**, though *pulverized* **(7)**, coffee beans. The more finely ground the coffee, the better the espresso. The process is made possible by espresso machines which heat the water, create the pressure, and release the "shot"—about 1.5 ounces. The espresso comes out syrupy in texture, murky brown in color, and with a *frothy* **(8)** layer at the top. To give the espresso a milder personality, you can combine a small amount of it with a pitcher of steamed or frothed hot milk to make *cappuccino*. **(9)** Now you're ready to order that cup of coffee which probably costs the *equivalent* **(10)** of a steak fajita dinner!

Practice 7: Word Games

A. **Word Bingo.** Make a list of 20 – 25 words based on this chapter's activities. Then create bingo cards for your group or the class. Each student writes one word randomly in each bingo square. Then teacher or student leader calls out clues or definitions for each word in any order. After a definition is called out, students find and cross out the matching word. As with any bingo game, the first to have a line of crossed off squares— vertically, horizontally, or diagonally—wins. The prize could be extra reading time or a gift certificate.

B. **Word Games.** You can also play versions of Password™, Concentration™, Word Rummy, or Pictionary™ based on words you develop from this chapter's activities. These games and their rules are available in retail stores.

C. **Computer Programs.** Some computer software programs allow you to create personalized word lists and/or games for learning various new words. Inquire at your local computer store. You can also download word games and exercises from the Internet. Share these exercises and games with your class for further practice.

D. **Words Around Us.** Find words you have seen or heard on radio, on television, in conversations, or in magazines. Bring the words to class with the sentences in which they were used. Do the words have prefixes, suffixes, or roots? Are there multiple meanings? Based on their definitions, what is the meaning of the words?

CONTEXT AND CONTEXT CLUES

We give names to ideas, events, objects and emotions. Often, however, there is no way to tell a word's meaning by the word alone. For example, consider the word "globe." There is nothing about the combination of the letters G-L-O-B-E to suggest the entire earth, yet everyone knows "the globe" used in any sense refers to a model of all the land, sea and sky on the planet.

To learn new words in a language, you need to have skills that allow you to decode what the word means. The most basic involves understanding how a word is used within a sentence and detecting the meaning from its use. When we understand the meaning of a sentence, we understand the ideas behind the words used, and as a consequence the words themselves. The words and ideas in the text surrounding a word are called the **context**. When put together, the context will reveal clues to the meaning of unfamiliar words.

Using **context clues** means looking at the way words are used in combination with other words in their setting. Look at the words *around* an unknown word. Think about the meaning of these words or the idea of the whole sentence. Then, match the meaning of the unknown word to the meaning of the known text.

In the following statements, choose the word which best reflects the meaning of the underlined word.

1. Many kinds of green algae remain <u>dormant</u> until rain revives them.

   A. dry   B. dead   C. small   D. inactive

2. <u>Aerobic</u> exercise increases your heart and breathing rates for a sustained period of time.

   A. of short duration   C. requiring oxygen

   B. improving strength   D. silly

By paying attention to context clues, we can determine that algae remain something *until rain revives them.* The opposite of "revive" is "to put to sleep." Therefore rain does something to bring the algae to life, to wake it up. Of the given choices, only *D* most closely resembles sleep. The other choices simply do not fit within the context or setting of ideas contained in the sentence.

Question 2 is a bit harder to figure out. The meaning of the word "aerobic" is called into question. We can rule out *A* because a sustained period of time would not agree with "of short duration." *B* seems pretty close, except that all exercise does not result in improved strength. Choice *D* is plainly not the answer, because the word "silly" doesn't fit the serious tone of the sentence; it was actually only included to make you laugh and to point out that context is frequently a source of humor. Finally, choice *C* is correct, because the definition "requiring oxygen" satisfies all the requirements of the sentence's context. It most perfectly fits the "setting" of the sentence.

Word Meaning

When you encounter an unfamiliar word or phrase in a sentence, consider the function of other words in the sentence. By looking at and analyzing the phrases and signal words that come before or after a particular word, you can often figure out an unknown word's meaning.

Context Clues	Signal Words
Comparison	*also, like, resembles, too, both, than* Look for clues that indicate an unfamiliar word is similar to a familiar word or phrase. **Example:** The accident felled the utility pole like a tree for timber.
Contrast	*but, however, while, instead of, yet, unlike* Look for clues that indicate an unfamiliar word is opposite in meaning to a familiar word or phrase. **Example:** Stephanie is usually in a state of *composure* while her sister is mostly boisterous.
Definition or Restatement	*is, or, that is, in other words, which* Look for words that define the term or restate it in other words. **Example:** The principal's idea is to *circuit* — or move around — the campus weekly to make sure everything is okay.
Example	*for example, for instance, such as* Look for examples used in context that reveal the meaning of an unfamiliar word. **Example:** People use all sorts of *vehicles* such as cars, bicycles, rickshaws, airplanes, boats, and motorcycles.

Practice 8: Context Clues

Above each underlined word, write its meaning. Use context clues to help you, referring if necessary to the chart above.

1. In the introductory course, she will study the <u>rudimentary</u> principles of chemistry.

2. The cure for the disease was discovered by a <u>pathologist</u> in Augusta.

3. Though he thought no one saw him, the little boy hid <u>conspicuously</u> beneath his blanket.

4. As a <u>corollary</u> principle to gravity, what goes up must come down.

5. The small deer peacefully drinking the river water was an <u>idyllic</u> scene to the hikers.

6. Most people think that ten-gallon hats are <u>endemic</u> to Texas.

7. The <u>notorious</u> gangster Al Capone was ultimately jailed for income tax fraud.

8. In a <u>peripatetic</u> manner, he walked around the mall from store to store.

9. Though his <u>predilection</u> was toward ice cream, Sam ordered a piece of chocolate cake.

10. The <u>paternal</u> instinct of the father made him protect his child from the escaped bear.

11. This word is <u>ambiguous</u>; it can have two meanings.

12. The <u>grandiose</u> dreams of Don Quixote led him to attack a field full of windmills.

13. The <u>prolific</u> actor has starred in four movies this year alone.

14. The landlord was <u>incensed</u> when he heard that there had been another arsonist fire.

15. The bad odor from the rotting beets <u>permeated</u> the entire house.

Working with context clues within essays will also provide valuable insight into word meanings.

Practice 9: More Context Practice

Read the following story, and then answer the questions which follow.

A Thief's Surprise

Andrea and her brother, Dan, arrived early that morning and parked their car near the parade route for the <u>annual</u> Duluth Christmas Parade. Many shops had closed along the parade route. Dan watched the parade <u>ardently</u>. He wanted to hear his school band perform the music they had worked on so <u>arduously</u> all semester. Meanwhile, Andrea went window shopping at the glass storefronts nearby. Suddenly, she noticed a flash of light off to her left. It came from the reflection of a man's watch. He was looking <u>intensely</u> into the music store window nearby.

Dan was listening <u>intently</u> as the school band marched by. The music was so loud it was deafening. At the same moment, Andrea glanced to the left and noticed the same man just before he used a sledgehammer to break through the glass window of the music store. In shock, Andrea ran to get her brother. She screamed, "Dan, come here!" However, he could not hear her above the sounds of the marching band. In <u>desperation</u>, she grabbed Dan from behind and turned him around.

"Dan, there is a man down the street who is robbing a music store!" she exclaimed.

Dan was the star wrestler on his school team and was ready to put his talents to good use. He ran as fast as he could and arrived at the music store just as the thief was coming out of the store. The thief was clutching an expensive electric guitar. Luckily for Dan, the thief did not have a gun. In an <u>expeditious</u> manner, Dan put the thief into a headlock and forced him to the sidewalk. By then, Andrea had found a police officer, who arrested the would-be <u>larcenist</u>.

1. Which of the following is closest in meaning to the word <u>annual</u>?
   A. daily
   B. monthly
   C. weekly
   D. yearly

2. In the context of the passage, which of the following is closest in meaning to the word <u>ardently</u>?
   A. with eagerness
   B. with boredom
   C. with integrity
   D. with anxiety

3. In this passage, which of the following is closest in meaning to the word <u>arduously</u>?
   A. long
   B. hard
   C. gracefully
   D. quickly

4. In this passage, which of the following is closest in meaning to the word <u>intensely</u>?
   A. with great hope
   B. with great distraction
   C. with great concentration
   D. with great enthusiasm

5. In this passage, which of the following is closest in meaning to the word <u>intently</u>?
   A. indifferently
   B. closely
   C. impassively
   D. unclearly

6. In this passage, which of the following is closest in meaning to the word <u>desperation</u>?
   A. joy
   B. extreme anger
   C. annoyance
   D. great anxiety

7. In this passage, which of the following is closest in meaning to the word <u>expeditious</u>?
   A. careful
   B. slow
   C. quick
   D. hesitant

8. In this passage, which of the following is closest in meaning to the word <u>larcenist</u>?
   A. thief
   B. mentor
   C. musician
   D. politician

Practice 10: Words in Context

Study the <u>underlined</u> words in their contexts. Guess at their meanings, and write your guess in the first blank. Then look up the word or phrase in your dictionary for the correct meaning. What context skills did you use?

1. The broken ankle of the star had a <u>deleterious</u> effect on the ability of the team.

a. (guess)_____

b. (dictionary)_____

2. The teacher <u>hypothesized</u> about the student's tardiness, but he could not prove it.

a. (guess)_____

b. (dictionary)_____

3. A <u>cursory</u> glance at the weather outside was disappointing, but a closer look revealed some sunshine breaking through in the distance.

a. (guess)_____

b. (dictionary)_____

CHAPTER 1 SUMMARY

Interpreting the words in a selection are important for understanding what you are reading.

- Learning **root words, prefixes**, and **suffixes** is one strategy for building your knowledge of words.

- The dictionary can also help you learn new words, their parts of speech, and their multiple meanings.

- Using **context clues** while you read is another effective way to understand the meaning of a passage.

CHAPTER 1 REVIEW

A. Use the sample dictionary selection to answer the questions below.

Sample Dictionary Page

366 dashboard - dastardly

dash•board *n.* a panel under the windshield of the vehicle, containing indicator dials, compartments, and sometimes control instruments. [Scand. origin]

da•sheen *n.* the taro (sense 2). [Orig. unknown]

dash•er *n.* **1.** One that dashes. **2.** The plunger of a churn or ice cream freezer. **3.** a spirited person.

da•shi•ki *n.* A loose, brightly colored African tunic, usually worn by men. [Yoruba origin]

dash•ing *adj.* **1.** Audacious and gallant; spirited. **2.** Marked by showy elegance; splendid. **da•shing•ly** *adv.*

dash•pot *n.* A piston-and-cylinder device used to damp motion.

das•sie *n.* The hyrax. [Afr. origin] dim. of das, badger [MDV]

das•tard *n.* A base, sneaking coward. [Middle English origin]

das•tard•ly *adj.* Cowardly and mean-spirited; base. **-das•tard•li•ness** *n.*

   Usage: *Dastardly* is employed most precisely when it combines the meaning of "vicious" and "cowardly." It is loosely used to mean simply "base" or "reprehensible." Thus, a gunman who shoots his victim in the back is committing a *dastardly* act.

---

1. What is the name for a brightly colored African tunic? _____

2. What is the adverb form of dashing? _____

3. What word would best describe a person who shoots someone in the back? _____

4. **Das** is a shorter form of which word? _____

5. What is the second definition for **dasher?** _____

B. Look Alikes - Sound Alikes. Look up each of the following words in a dictionary. Identify the part(s) of speech, the various meanings, and then use each word in a sentence:

affect	allusion	capital	cite
effect	illusion	capitol	site
conscious	desert	device	elicit
conscience	dessert	devise	illicit
heard	loose	passed	personal
herd	lose	past	personnel
principal	stationary	than	threw
principle	stationery	then	through

C. Words to Know. How many of these words do you know? Find out their meanings and parts of speech. See if you can use them in a sentence:

anticipate	gratify	narrate	urban	bilingual	hybrid
ordeal	visualize	concoct	induce	prism	wean
divert	jovial	replica	zest	essence	khaki
spontaneous	flagrant				

D. Personal Word List. To improve your knowledge of words, create a personal word list. Divide pages in your notebook into four columns. For each word entry, list the word (1) followed by the pronunciation and part of speech (2), the use of the word in a sentence (3), and finally the dictionary definition (4). As you find new words, add them to your personal word list, and review them periodically. Use the chart below as a model.

Sample Personal Word Entry			
Word	**Pronunciation/ Part of Speech**	**Use in Sentence**	**Definition**
surname	sur´ nam v.n	Her surname is Smith.	family name, last name
annual	an´ yoo wel adj	New Year's Eve is an annual celebration in the United States.	once a year, yearly

Word Meaning

E. Word Meanings And Context Clues. Read the following article. Then answer the questions that follow.

What Is Ethics, Anyway?

Ethics is a concept we hear about, but few people today stop to think what it really means. However, philosophers and statesmen since the time of Plato have **contemplated** the definition and details of ethics, which is sometimes difficult to state. Clearly, ethics is not something invented by one person or even a society, but has some well-founded standards on which it is based.

Some people **equate** ethics with feelings. But being ethical is not simply following one's feelings. A criminal may "feel" robbing a person is okay, when really it is wrong and unethical to steal. Many people may identify ethics with religion, and it is true that most religions include high ethical standards and strong motivation for people to behave morally. But ethics cannot be confined only to religion, or only religious people could be ethical. There are even cases in which religious teaching and ethics clash: for example, some religions **inhibit** the rights of women, which opposes the ethical standard of basic justice.

Ethics also is not simply following laws or what is accepted by a society. The laws of civilized nations often **embody** ethical standards. However, unethical laws can exist. For example, laws have allowed slavery, which is unethical behavior as it takes the freedom of another human being. Therefore, laws and other conventions accepted by a society cannot be the measure for what is ethical. Doing "whatever society accepts" may be far outside the realm of ethics — Nazi Germany is an example of an ethically **debased** society.

What ethics really refers to is a system of people's moral standards and values. It's like a road map of qualities that people want to have to be "decent human beings." It is also the formal study of the standards of human behavior. Ethics relies on well-based standards of "right" (like honesty, compassion, and loyalty) and "wrong" (like stealing, murder, and fraud). Ethical standards **encompass** ideas such as respect for others, honesty, justice, doing good, and preventing harm.

1. In the context of this passage, what does the word <u>contemplated</u> mean?
   - A. thought about
   - B. looked at
   - C. taken apart
   - D. examined

2. In the context of this passage, which of the following is closest in meaning to <u>equate</u>?
   - A. compare
   - B. multiply
   - C. balance
   - D. flatten

3. In this passage, which of the following is closest in meaning to the word <u>inhibit</u>?
   - A. lie about
   - B. live in
   - C. give in to
   - D. hold back

4. 12. Which dictionary definition of the word <u>debased</u> best applies to its use in the passage?
   - A. depraved
   - B. corrupt
   - C. impure
   - D. distorted

5. In this passage, which of the following is closest in meaning to the word <u>encompass</u>?
   - A. steer
   - B. include
   - C. begin
   - D. mean

© Copyright American Book Company. DO NOT DUPLICATE. 1-888-264-5877.

Chapter 2
Details, Main Ideas, and Summarizing

This chapter covers Minnesota Reading Standard(s):

1.C.1	Students will summarize and paraphrase main ideas and supporting details.

Locating details, finding the main idea, and summarizing what you read are important strategies for understanding fiction and nonfiction. In this chapter, you will learn and practice each of these strategies.

The first strategy you will learn about is locating details in a reading selection. An author writes to communicate with the reader and to share a message, information, or idea. To help you understand what the author is saying, he or she will answer the **5 Ws and an H**: the Who, What, Where, Why, When, and How in the story or article. These are all helpers in showing you, the reader, the purpose of the story or article. Knowing the importance of these details will also help you with the process of **summarizing**, condensing information for study, or responses to questions about text materials.

The 5 Ws and an H help you to understand what you are reading and help in your writing too. They are constant companions and guides to a writer's essays, narratives, short stories, or research papers.

THE FIVE WS AND AN H

- Who is the story or article about?

- What is the point or idea of the text? What is the reason the author is writing the story or article?

- Where does the plot or main idea take place?

- Why is the main idea important? Why is the main character acting this way?

- When does the story or article take place?

- How does the author reveal a motive or a reason?

These and other questions must be answered to understand a story or article.

Details and facts answer these questions and give color and meaning to the writing. The main idea is what drives the story or article. Details support the main idea.

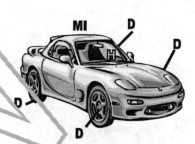

Think of an automobile. Without tires, an engine, and a steering wheel, the car would not work.

In the same way, it would be impossible to understand what the author is trying to say without facts and details to support the main idea of a story or article.

LOCATING DETAILS

An author uses details to help you understand what you are reading. Details can be people, places, and things. They can be facts, explanations, and reasons too. They all answer the 5 Ws and the H.

Finding the facts and details is sometimes easy and sometimes challenging.

Read the paragraph below, and see if you can find the answers to the questions that follow.

A Classic Car Story

Sterling McCall began collecting cars in 1979 in a small Texas town. A Toyota customer drove a 1927 Ford Model T Doctor's Coupe into his dealership. The customer wanted to trade it for a new car. The Ford Model T was so unique and fun to drive Mr. McCall gladly made a deal. He liked the antique car so much he decided not to sell it and kept it in a barn on his farm outside of Houston.

Mr. McCall's hobby of collecting older model cars became the talk of the town. People began to bring their old cars to the dealership to trade for a new car. In 15 years, Mr. McCall collected so many classic and antique cars he had to build garages all over his farm. A 1941 Buick Convertible, a 1948 Lincoln Continental convertible, and a 1946 Plymouth convertible were a few of the valuable and rare classics Mr. McCall bought, restored, and drove just for fun.

The collection of cars totaled 88 when Mr. McCall finally decided to stop building garages on his farm and to open a car museum in Warrenton, a town located three miles from his farm. The Sterling McCall Old Car Museum opened in 1998. The museum provides a glimpse into the history of the automobile.

1. Who is the story about?
   A. Sterling McCall
   B. Toyota customers
   C. car mechanic
   D. the mayor of Warrenton

2. What was the first car in Mr. Sterling's collection?
   A. Buick convertible
   B. Lincoln Continental
   C. Lexus
   D. Model T

3. Where was the car collection kept by the end of the story?
   A. Houston   B. on a farm   C. a museum in Warrenton   D. Galveston

4. When did Mr. Sterling start his collection?

   A. 1976   B. 1988   C. 1998   D. 1979

5. Why did Mr. Sterling open a museum?

   A. He did not want people visiting his farm.
   B. He wanted to get the cars off his road.
   C. He did not want to build any more garages.
   D. He did not like cars anymore.

6. How did Mr. Sterling make a living?

   A. collecting cars   B. as a farmer   C. as a mechanic   D. selling cars

Questions 1–3 are easy to answer because the facts are written plainly in the text. Questions 4–6 require a more careful reading. All the choices in question 6 could be correct, but D is the best answer, since Mr. Sterling owned a car dealership. Nothing in the passage clearly says that he made money from the other three choices.

Tips for Locating Details

1. **Read the question carefully,** and be sure you understand what is being asked.

2. **If you are unsure of the answer,** go back to the text and read to find the details.

3. **Eliminate obvious wrong answers first.** Then find the detail that points to the right answer.

4. **Make sure to review** your answers after finishing the questions.

Practice 1: Locating Details

Read the paragraph below, and answer the questions that follow. Write in complete sentences.

Students at the Pine Hill Elementary School in Minnesota were in for a treat. Third grade student Dirk Collins was going to talk with his father on a ham radio in the cafeteria. Not impressed? His father is International Space Station Expedition 8 Commander Mike Collins. The commander had been living on the International Space Station with Russian Flight Engineer Ivan Kozov for several months. Commander Collins told the students that from the window of the space station he could see snow on the mountains and mud in the rivers of Earth. The crew could not see the pyramids in Egypt or the Great Wall of China because they blended with their surroundings. Amateur Radio sponsored the event on the International Space Station (ARISS) program.

1. Who did the students listen to from space?

2. What could the astronaut see out the window of the space station?

3. Where does the conversation take place?

4. When did the commander go into space?

5. Why couldn't the astronauts see the Great Wall of China?

6. How did the students communicate with the commander?

Practice 2: Locating Details

Now it is your turn to ask questions as you look for details.

Read the passage below from "The Story of Dr. Dolittle," written by Hugh Lofting in 1922. Create questions that have a What? Where? Who? When? Why? and How? in them about the passage.

Don't forget to answer the questions, and then trade questions with your classmates to see if you get the same answers.

Excerpt from "Dr. Dolittle"
by Hugh Lofting

Once upon a time, many years ago, when our grandfathers were little children, there was a doctor; and his name was Dolittle — John Dolittle, M.D. "M.D." means that he was a proper doctor and knew a whole lot....

He was very fond of animals and kept many kinds of pets. Besides the goldfish in the pond at the bottom of his garden, he had rabbits in the pantry, white mice in his piano, a squirrel in the linen closet, and a hedgehog in the cellar. He had a cow with a calf too, and an old lame horse — twenty-five years of age — and chickens, and pigeons, and two lambs, and many other animals. But his favorite pets were Dab-Dab the duck, Jip the dog, Gub-Gub the baby pig, Polynesia the parrot, and the owl Too-Too.

Now, you are ready to write the 5 Ws and H questions. You may refer to the passage as you create your questions.

THE MAIN IDEA

Read the following sentence: "The **main idea** or central point can be found in two different ways." That sentence is a good example of a topic sentence—it says in a broad statement what this paragraph will be about. "Topic" is another word for subject. Main ideas are *broad statements* about the subject of a paragraph or passage. Details of a passage support this statement. Statements of details alone cannot be main ideas. Look below for the two ways main ideas may be found:

1) Sometimes main ideas may be **directly stated** in a topic sentence; topic sentences can be found in the title, the introduction, and even a beginning sentence or ending sentence of a paragraph. They are almost never found in the middle of a passage. Sometimes the main idea of a passage may be found in the title. In the example of the topic sentence above, that is where you will find the main idea of the paragraph.

2) Another way an author shows the reader the main idea is by implying, hinting, or suggesting the main idea through the details and facts in a passage, and not by directly stat-

ing it. This is called an **implied main idea**. The reader really has to be a detective and look for clues in the details.

To review, there are two ways authors reveal the main idea:

1. **A statement or phrase of a directly stated main idea, and**

2. **A statement that implies the main idea.**

Now let's practice discovering the main idea.

A DIRECTLY STATED MAIN IDEA

When you read information with a directly stated main idea, you will usually find some or all of the main idea in the title, in the beginning sentence, or in the ending sentences.

The example below shows a directly stated main idea in the first sentence.

Mockingbirds are common and popular birds in the eastern and southern regions of the United States. The mockingbird is the state bird for Arkansas, Florida, Mississippi, Tennessee, and Texas. "Mockers," as they are affectionately called, are known for their ability to mimic other birds, mammals, and insects with song and sounds. Mockingbirds often live close to human homes, nesting in ornamental hedges.

After reading the first sentence, we know that the passage is about mockingbirds. The rest of the sentences give details about how the mockingbird is common and why it is popular. Read the next two passages and their questions. An explanation for the correct answer is found after each set of questions.

Modern-Day Wonder

The title of "modern-day wonder of the world" really should go to the Smithsonian Institution. It is the largest grouping of museums and art galleries in the world. You will find "the Smithsonian," the name most people call it, in the heart of the nation's capital, Washington, D.C. The Smithsonian is near all the major federal government buildings, such as the White House. The Smithsonian has more than 100 million objects and specimens in its collections. It is said to take weeks to see everything in the collections. The objects range from the funny to the unique. You may see, for example, George Washington's false teeth, the Inauguration gowns of the First Ladies, and the Apollo Lunar Landing Module. As if that were not enough, the Smithsonian also has a zoo with more than 2,000 animals in it. The National Zoological Park and the National Air and Space Museum are two of the favorite attractions in the Smithsonian Institution. Most of the 13 museums and art galleries are located next to each other in an area called The Mall. This collection of human knowledge and experience is truly a wonder.

Details, Main Ideas, and Summarizing

1. What is the main idea of the paragraph?

   A.   The zoo and the air and space museum are the most popular attractions in the Smithsonian.

   B.   George Washington's false teeth are on display at the Smithsonian.

   C.   The Smithsonian Institution has the largest group of museums and art galleries in the world.

   D.   The Smithsonian Institution is located in the heart of downtown Washington, D.C.

Choice C is correct: The main idea is directly stated near the beginning of the passage. Choices A, B, and D are all details that support the main idea. Remember the example of the car supported by its wheels.

Excerpt from *The Prince and the Pauper*
by Mark Twain

> In the ancient city of London, on a certain autumn day in the second quarter of the sixteenth century, a boy was born to a poor family of the name of Canty, who did not want him. On the same day, another English child was born to a rich family of the name of Tudor, who did want him. All England wanted him too. England had so longed for him, and hoped for him, and prayed God for him, that, now that he was really come, the people went nearly mad for joy.

2. What is the main idea of this paragraph?

   A.   In London, a baby boy was born to the poor Canty family during the fall of the year.

   B.   London is an ancient city in England.

   C.   The Tudor family was wealthy and well liked.

   D.   A prince and a pauper were born on the same day in very different circumstances.

The main idea is directly stated in the title. Choice D correctly describes what the passage is about. Choices A, B, and C describe only parts of the main idea.

Tips for Finding a Stated Main Idea

1. Read the title. The main topic of the paragraph or passage is often mentioned in the title.

2. Read the first and last sentence of each paragraph. Most of the key words and ideas will be stated in these places.

3. Choose the answer that is the best statement or restatement of the paragraph or passage. Your choice should contain the key words mentioned in the title, the first sentence, or the last sentence of each paragraph or passage.

4. Always read the entire passage to get an overview of what the author is writing.

AN IMPLIED MAIN IDEA

An author can give you important information without directly stating it, by giving clues or suggestions through the details of the passage. Be a detective, and see what the clues in the following sentence tell you.

Sam's favorite part of the hike was watching the colorful leaves falling all around him.

What season of the year is it? The author does not say, but you can figure it out. You can conclude that the season is autumn because of the hints the author gives you. Because the season is described without using the word "autumn," it is **implied**.

Does Sam enjoy hiking? The author doesn't say it directly, but you can come to the conclusion that he does enjoy hiking since there is a "favorite part" to the hike. The author *implies* that Sam enjoyed the hike.

An implied main idea can be found by reading more than one sentence and looking for clues. In a paragraph, you will be reading several sentences. If there is no directly stated main idea, you will need to think of the sentences as answers to the 5 W's and H. The implied main idea will be a broad statement supported by these answers—like the car supported and steered by wheels. Read the following passage, and try to look for the implied main idea.

Traveling the Speed of Light

In 1905, a scientist named Albert Einstein published the first of his two famous theories: the Special Theory of Relativity. The theory states that the faster an object travels, the heavier it becomes. Therefore, an object traveling at 300,000 kilometers a second or the speed of light would be extremely heavy. The theory also connects the speed of light with the passage of time. Einstein believed everything in the universe is connected and that traveling the speed of light would slow time down. Light is the fastest thing known to science. If scientists can figure out a way to travel the speed of light, they would be able to discover whether the theory is true or false. Most scientists consider Albert Einstein a genius.

Albert Einstein

1. What is the implied main idea in this paragraph?

    A.   Albert Einstein may be the smartest man who ever lived.

    B.   The Special Theory of Relativity is still an important and puzzling theory for scientists.

    C.   The speed of light is the fastest thing known to man.

    D.   A rocket ship might weigh a lot more if it traveled the speed of light.

The title suggests the subject of the passage is the speed of light but does not give the reader enough information to conclude what the main idea of the paragraph is. It is only after we read the entire paragraph that we understand what the main idea is.

Choice A is an implied detail but does not convey the main idea. Choices C and D are directly stated details that do not convey the main idea. Choice B is the implied main point of the story, which is supported by the other details.

IMPLIED MAIN IDEAS IN PASSAGES OF SEVERAL PARAGRAPHS

You may be asked to read passages that have several paragraphs. You will need to read more than one paragraph to discover what the main idea is in the passage. In some of these long passages, the main idea may be directly stated in the title, first sentence, or last sentence. However, if the main idea is not directly stated, you will need to carefully read the details of each paragraph. The implied main idea will be a combination of these details and facts.

Read the passage below to practice your detecting skills as you look for and note the details. See if you can "read between the lines" and find the implied main idea in this passage.

Tourism as an Industry

Have you ever traveled to another city or country? If you have, then you were a tourist. Tourism is popular everywhere from small towns to large countries. It is one of the world's largest industries, and in many regions, it is the only source of money and jobs.

While tourism does not have the same 'bad guy' image as the manufacturing industry, it is not an environmentally friendly business. Tourism creates pollution and consumes natural resources.

The United States is a favorite tourist destination of people from all over the world. It faces the challenge of making its tourist industry less damaging to the environment and natural resources. The tourism industry will be harmed if people do not visit because of polluted beaches or a littered countryside.

In the passage above, the title, the first sentence, and last sentence do not directly state the main idea of the passage. They reveal only the subject. You have to read through all the paragraphs and note the details to understand completely what the author is saying.

2. What is the implied main idea?

    A. Being a tourist in another country can be fun and educational.

    B. The tourism industry can make money.

    C. Tourism can be a harmful industry to the environment.

    D. The tourism industry brings welcome money and unwelcome problems to countries.

Choice A is incorrect because the author is not concerned with how much fun a tourist has. Choices B and C are direct statements that are correct but do not state the main idea. Choice D is the implied main idea of the passage. The author does not directly state the sentence in answer D, but through examples and details, the reader can conclude that the tourism industry provides both advantages and disadvantages to a country.

Tips for Determining an Implied Main Idea

1. **Read the title and first sentence.** Both will help you identify the topic of the selection.

2. **Read the entire paragraph or passage.** You'll get a general understanding of the selection.

3. **Note the facts and details** in each paragraph. Think of overall ideas they share in common.

4. **Choose the answer that summarizes** all of the facts and ideas in the passage. Confirm your choice by going back to the passage to check your evidence one more time.

Practice 3: Main Idea in a Paragraph

Read each of the following paragraphs. Decide whether the main idea is stated or implied. If the main idea is stated, underline it. If the main idea is implied, write it in your own words in the space provided. Discuss your answers with your classmates and teacher.

A Visit to Germany

In Germany, lunch is the main meal for most families. Supper is a cold meal which resembles a light American lunch. Potatoes are a favorite dish. They are cooked in many ways and with different spices. Germans also like to eat sausage, or "wurst." Fresh bread rolls are stuffed with wurst for a snack. Some kinds of food, like seafood, may be difficult to find in most restaurants in Germany, but the hundreds of varieties of wursts make meals interesting and tasty.

1. _____

_____

Feeding the Fish

Fishermen at Lake Chickasaw were puzzled. They weren't catching the bass and stripers as successfully as they had last summer. They tried all sorts of lures and hooks, but nothing seemed to help. The fish they did catch were small and bony. A biologist studied the lake and found that the fish were starving. They had nothing to eat. She told the fishermen to stock the lake with minnows, a small fish usually used as bait. The following year, the bass and stripers were healthy, and the fishermen were happy.

2. _____

_____

Details, Main Ideas, and Summarizing

How to Make a Pizza

It is easy to order pizza, but you can make one too. A telephone call, $20, and a parent's nod of approval can deliver a succulent pizza to your door. But did you know that making your own pizza could be just as delicious and more fun? Pizza crusts are sold at most grocery stores, and you only need Italian tomato sauce, mozzarella cheese, and a little imagination.

3. _____

_____

Passing a Test

It was the day Claire had been waiting for all summer long. She would be tested as a swimmer. Claire had learned to swim by taking lessons at the beach. Strokes of the arm, kicking the legs rapidly, and swimming like a frog were all the mechanics she had practiced. As Claire swam the half-mile required for her test, a small boat, commandeered by her instructor, followed her. It was a test of endurance.

4. _____

_____

A Golden Seal

In 1922, the Newbery Award became the first children's book award in the world. The award is named after an eighteenth-century English bookseller, John Newbery. In the library or media center, you can find the books that have won this important award. A bright gold seal is printed on the cover of all winning books. It is the best known and most discussed children's book award in the country.

_____

_____

Practice 4: Main Ideas in Passages

In the following passages, the main idea is either directly stated or implied. If the main idea is stated, underline it. If the main idea is implied, write it in your own words in the space provided. Discuss your answers with the class or instructor.

How Important Is Oil?

There is a big debate in this country that centers on a wildlife refuge in the United States.

The Arctic National Wildlife Refuge is the second largest wildlife refuge in the United States. It is 19 million acres in size and is located in the northeast corner of Alaska. The refuge is home to all sorts of animals and birds, including caribou, grizzly bears, polar bears, and oxen.

The refuge is also home to one of the largest oil reserves in the country. Some people think of the refuge as a beautiful place that should be protected. Drilling for oil could cause harm to the animals, the coastal waters, and the natural habitat. Other people think that our country needs the oil and that Alaskans would benefit from the jobs drilling for oil would give them.

1. _____

_____

A Field Trip to the Museum

The students were excited. It was their first field trip of the year. As the school bus parked, the children watched a large outdoor Calder sculpture slowly turn in the breeze.

Inside the museum, century-old paintings hung on the gallery walls. One painting showed a silver teapot and pastries glimmering on a very heavy silver tray. One woman in the painting looked thoughtful, and the other woman sipped tea.

Other paintings showed mountains, boats, and flowers.

Time went by fast, and soon it was time to leave.

"Alright, children, it's time to move on," said Mr. Smith, the teacher. "So many artists, so little time. The school buses won't wait for us forever."

2. _____

_____

Composting a Garden

Leaves, coffee grounds, and orange skins have a lot in common when it comes to composting. All are organic, and, when they are left to decompose in a compost pile, they become vitamins for the soil.

In forests, jungles, and gardens, plants die and decay. Eventually, they disappear and become humus. Humus is dark in color, lightweight and fluffy soil, which is very good for vegetable plants, flowers, and trees. Sometimes humus is called topsoil. Composting gives the gardener humus.

Most gardeners have long understood the value of composting. It is the best way to add healthy materials to the soil.

3. _____

_____

Details, Main Ideas, and Summarizing

Sailing the Seas

Christopher Columbus was born in Genoa, Italy. As a boy, Christopher attended the University of Pavia, where he studied grammar, geometry, geography, navigation, astronomy, and Latin. He graduated school at the age of 14 and began his life as a young seaman.

"I went to sea from the most tender age and have continued in a sea life to this day," Columbus wrote in his journal.

Columbus sailed the seas for more than 40 years and was proud of his accomplishments. One day he wrote in his journal, "Wherever any one has sailed, there I have sailed."

4. _____

_____

Weather Facts

Rain develops when cloud droplets become too heavy to remain in the cloud and fall toward the surface of the earth as rain. Rain can also begin as ice crystals that stick to each other to form snowflakes. As the falling snow passes through the freezing level into warmer air, the flakes melt into raindrops.

Hail is a large frozen raindrop produced by strong thunderstorms. It can damage cars and homes. Hail begins as snowflakes. As the snowflakes fall, liquid water freezes onto them forming ice pellets. The pellets continue to grow in size as more and more droplets are accumulated. The ice pellets are bounced back to the top of the storm cloud by strong "updrafts," and the process repeats itself. Hail can be larger than a golf ball.

5. _____

_____

Practice 5:   Main Ideas in Passages

On your own or with your classmates, read other passages from the diagnostic test. Are the main ideas stated or implied? If they are stated, underline them. If they are implied, write the main idea in your own words. Then share your findings with the class or the instructor.

Practice 6:   Media Search for Main Ideas

A. **Idea Exchange.** On your own or in a group, look for paragraphs and passages on different subjects in newspapers, magazines, books, or the Internet. Write out the stated or implied main ideas you find on a separate sheet of paper. Bring the articles to class. Exchange only the articles with another student or group members. See if they identify the same main ideas that you did. Then share the results of your efforts with your instructor.

B. **Photo Titles.** Share photos or pictures with a partner. Then think of titles or main ideas to go with them.

C. **News Story Headlines.** Bring news stories to class. Cut out the headlines, and keep them separate. Exchange only the articles, and write your own headlines. Compare your own headlines with the original headlines.

SUMMARIZING

Often while you are reading research material, you may want to make some written notes but may not want to use actual quotes from a source. In order to capture the main idea and supporting details from a source, it is very helpful to write a summary. A summary condenses the ideas in a source and allows you to use the ideas as a reference without having to reread the entire source each time. Writing a summary is also a good study tool that can be helpful when you have a great deal of reading to do.

Of course, the first step in writing a summary is to **read the entire article or source**. After reading through very carefully, make a list of brief notes which will serve as a framework for creating the summary. **Write down the subject of the article.** Next, **write down the main idea.** It is a good idea to go ahead and put it in complete sentence form. Now, **list the major details.** These don't have to be in complete sentences; phrases are sufficient. As you list these details, briefly **explain any unfamiliar terms or concepts** as necessary. Be sure that you use quotation marks to indicate exact words or phrases from the original source, but use quotations very sparingly, if you use them at all.

The first sentence of your summary should include the title of the source and the author. Now **write the summary in the form of a paragraph** using the notes you just created. Remember to use your own words; don't use phrases from the original unless absolutely necessary. As much as possible, a summary should be in your own words.

How long should your summary be? A general rule is to try and keep it to about one-fourth to one-third of the original length. So, if your original article were two pages long, a summary should be about one-half to about three-fourths of a page.

In this next section, read the article; read the notes the student made, and then read the summary of the article.

Why You Need a Compost Pile in Your Backyard
by Ben Sniffelmeyer

The home compost pile is an efficient mulch factory, and mulch is very valuable in the garden. Your garden will look more attractive, weeds will be smothered out, moisture can be conserved, and soil temperature fluctuations will happen less. Mulch can also be used to disguise bare dirt in the garden.

Since the process of plant matter decomposing into mulch takes time, gardeners usually have several compost piles "cooking" at various stages of decomposition. Rather than putting grass clippings and leaves in the landfill, they can be composted and recycled back into your garden as mulch. Chemical fertilizers put on the lawn and absorbed by the grass then get recycled through the reuse of the grass clippings. A compost pile also gains from some types of kitchen waste such as potato and carrot peelings, coffee grounds, and egg shells. Putting those items in a compost pile is more ecologically friendly than sending them to the sewage system by way of the garbage disposal or making them a part of the local landfill. Avoid adding meat to your compost pile. Otherwise, you will attract scavengers like rats and dogs.

A healthy compost pile attracts worms, and the more worms the better. Some gardeners new to composting are unhappy to see earthworms in their compost pile. Gardeners, you need to realize that those worms are very beneficial to the health of your garden soil because of their help in the decomposition of the vegetable and paper material. Remember, anything that is added to the compost pile becomes worm food.

A backyard compost pile will take some work and patience, but the rewards and benefits are well worth the time you will invest in getting it started and maintaining it.

Student Notes

Subject: backyard compost piles

Main idea: If you have a home garden, creating your own compost pile is easy, and the mulch produced is helpful.

Major details: may need more than one— garden plant waste is put to good use, not filling up the landfills—benefits of mulch: attractive, weed control, water holding, insulation for soil— worms attracted to the pile are "very beneficial to the health of your garden" and to the compost pile

Summary

The article "Why You Need a Compost Pile in Your Backyard" by Ben Spiffelmeyer discusses backyard compost piles. He says if you have a home garden, creating your own compost pile is easy, and the mulch produced is helpful. Having a compost pile allows garden plant waste to be put to good use, not to fill up the landfills. Home gardeners may need more than one pile since the process takes time. Four benefits are listed: (1) mulch can improve the appearance of your garden; (2) mulch will help control weeds; (3) the mulch helps gardens retain moisture; (4) it also helps insulate the soil from heat and cold weather. You need and want the worms that will appear in the pile since they help the composting process.

Practice 7: Summarizing

A. Write notes and a summary for the following passage.

Excerpt from "Walking" by Henry David Thoreau

My vicinity affords many good walks; and though for so many years I have walked almost every day, and sometimes for several days together, I have not yet exhausted them. An absolutely new prospect is a great happiness, and I can still get this any afternoon. Two or three hours' walking will carry me to as strange a country as I expect ever to see. A single farmhouse which I had not seen before is sometimes as good as the dominions of the King of Dahomey. There is in fact a sort of harmony discoverable between the capabilities of the landscape within a circle of ten miles' radius, or the limits of an afternoon walk, and the threescore years and ten of human life. It will never become quite familiar to you.

Section deleted

I can easily walk ten, fifteen, twenty, any number of miles, commencing at my own door, without going by any house, without crossing a road except where the fox and mink do: first along by the river, and then the brook, and then the meadow and the woodside. There are square miles in my vicinity which have no inhabitant. From many a hill I can see civilization and the abodes of man afar. The farmers and their works are scarcely more obvious than woodchucks and their burrows. Man and his affairs, church and state and school, trade and commerce, and manufactures and agriculture, even politics, the most alarming of them all, I am pleased to see how little space they occupy in the landscape. Politics is but a narrow field, and that still narrower highway yonder leads to it. I sometimes direct the traveller thither. If you would go into the political world, follow the great road, follow that market-man, keep his dust in your eyes, and it will lead you straight to it; for it, too, has its place merely, and does not occupy all space. I pass from it as from a beanfield into the forest, and it is forgotten. In one half-hour I can walk off to some portion of the earth's surface where a man does not stand from one year's end to another, and there, politics are not, for they are but as the cigar-smoke of man.

B. Find two articles of 1 – 2 pages from newspapers or magazines, and write summaries of them. If you have a research project that you are now working on for a class, your teacher may let you use articles from that research. Trade articles and summaries with a partner, and comment on each other's summaries.

CHAPTER 2 SUMMARY

- Locating **details,** finding the **main idea**, and **summarizing** information are key strategies for understanding what you are reading.

- Use the **five Ws and H** to help you locate important details.

- Main ideas can be **stated directly** or **implied** in a reading selection.

- When you are locating a **main idea**, pay attention to the title, the first and last part of the passage, and the supporting details.

- Writing a **summary** is good practice for improving understanding and studying for classes and tests.

CHAPTER 2 REVIEW

Read the following passages, and answer the questions that follow each passage. List two supporting details in each passage. Compare your answers with your classmates.

Excerpt from *The Red-Headed League* by Conan Doyle

Our visitor bore every mark of being an average commonplace British tradesman, obese, pompous, and slow. He wore rather baggy gray shepherd's check trousers, a not over-clean black frock-coat, unbuttoned in the front, and a drab waistcoat with a heavy brassy Albert chain, and a square pierced bit of metal dangling down as an ornament. A frayed top hat and a faded brown overcoat with a wrinkled velvet collar lie upon a chair beside him. Altogether, look as I would, there was nothing remarkable about the man save his blazing red head, and the expression of extreme chagrin and discontent upon his features.

1. What is the main idea of the passage?

2. Is the main idea implied or directly stated?

3. Does the title state what the main idea is?

About Austin

Austin, located in central Texas, is the state capital. The city is located on terraced bluffs along a bend in the Colorado River, about 160 miles west of Houston. Austin is located in Travis County and is where the governor of the state lives. The city became the capital of the Republic of Texas in 1839. It became the state capital when Texas joined the Union in 1845. Austin has many famous attractions including the Lady Bird Johnson Wildflower Center and the Texas Ranger Hall of Fame and Museum.

4. What is the main idea of the passage?

5. Is the main idea implied or directly stated?

6. Does the title help the reader find the main idea?

Excerpt from *The Education of Henry Adams* by Henry Adams

Under the shadow of Boston State House, the little passage called Hancock Avenue runs, or ran, from Beacon Street, skirting the State House grounds, to Mount Vernon Street, on the summit of Beacon Hill; and there, in the third house below Mount Vernon Place, February 16, 1838, a child was born, and christened later by his uncle, as Henry Brooks Adams.

7. What city is the author describing?

8. What is the main idea?

9. Is the main idea implied or directly stated?

The Beginning of Transportation

The first road vehicles were two-wheeled carts built with crude stone disks that functioned like wheels. Used by the Sumerians around 3000 BC, the simple wagons resembled the chariot, which the Egyptians and Greeks developed from a crude lumbering cart into a work of beauty. In 1100 BC, the Chinese constructed the world's first permanent road system. In Asia, camels served to transport goods and people; elsewhere, oxen and burros were the beasts of burden. Later in the history of transportation, the Romans built 53,000 miles of roads, mostly for their armies.

10. What is the main idea?

11. Does the author imply or directly state the main idea in the passage?

12. How does the author reveal the main idea?

Excerpt From the Essay "On Drawing," by A.P. Herbert

It is commonly said that everybody can sing in the bathroom; and this is true. Singing is very easy. Drawing, though, is much more difficult. I have devoted a good deal of time to drawing, one way and another; I have to attend a great many committees and public meetings, and at such functions I find that drawing is almost the only Art one can satisfactorily pursue during the speeches. One really cannot sing during the speeches; so as a rule I draw. I do not say that I am an expert yet, but after a few more meetings I calculate that I shall know drawing as well as it can be known.

13. What is the main idea?

14. Is the main idea implied or directly stated?

15. What type of drawing is implied in the passage?

Going Up?

Soon after the hot-air balloon was invented in 1783, attempts were made to control the balloon's flight. Although sails, paddles, and flapping wings were tried, propellers proved to be the most suitable form of propulsion. The French inventor Henri Giffard built a steam-powered airship around the year 1852. However, it was not until the invention of the gasoline engine in 1896 that airships became practical. In 1898, the Brazilian Alberto Santon-Dumont was the first to construct and fly a gasoline-powered airship.

16. Does the first sentence state the main idea?

17. Is the main idea implied or directly stated?

18. Where does the author reveal the main idea?

A Look Back at Chocolate

Do you like chocolate? If you do, you are in luck. The United States has the largest chocolate manufacturing industry in the world. Everything from nuts to soup can be bought with chocolate in it.

The chocolate business did not begin in the United States. Aztecs in South America made a chocolate beverage thousands of years ago. In the year 1500, Spanish explorers brought beans grown from a chocolate tree in South America to Europe. There, chocolate liquid made from the plant became very popular as a drink.

In 1657, a shop opened in London where chocolate was sold at luxury prices. It became a fashionable drink, and shops sprang up as places to meet, drink chocolate, and talk politics. Chocolate was first manufactured in the United States in the state of Massachusetts in 1765. About 100 years later, a man in Switzerland perfected a process of making milk chocolate by combining cocoa, sugar, fat, and condensed milk. Today we have thousands of choices of things to eat that are made with chocolate.

19. What is the main idea of the passage?

20. Is there one sentence that gives you the central point, or did you have to read through the article?

21. Is the main idea directly stated or implied?

22. Write a summary of the chocolate passage. Include the main idea and supporting details.

Chapter 3
Making Inferences and Drawing Conclusions

This chapter covers Minnesota Reading Standard(s):

I.C.4	Students will make inferences and draw conclusions based on explicit and implied information from text.

Good readers are like detectives. They are able to pick out the clues left by an author and determine what is happening and will happen in a text. When readers make **inferences** and **conclusions**, they use their experiences and prior knowledge to understand what they are reading.

For example, you might walk into your classroom and see a notice on the board saying that today's English test is postponed. Knowing that your English teacher had mentioned feeling bad the day before and knowing that substitute teachers do not administer tests, you can make an educated guess. You may infer from the message and from knowledge of earlier events that the English teacher is ill and will not be in. We make these kinds of inferences every day. An **inference** is an educated guess based on information given in a text, clues in the text, and previous experience and knowledge.

If you were to make an inference based on this graphic, what could you infer? You might make the **inference** that the rodeo clown had better stay behind the barrel. You have guessed this based on the bull's facial expression and closeness to the barrel. You have made the **conclusion** that now is not a good time for the clown to leave the protection of the barrel.

You also make inferences when you read. Authors do not always directly state what they want you to understand. When you make an inference, you are noticing relevant details and clues in a text and then combining those clues with what you already know. This allows you to figure out events in a story.

For an example, read this passage from Richard Connell's "The Most Dangerous Game," and see if you can tell or infer what has happened to the character at the end.

Rainsford sprang up and moved quickly to the rail, mystified. He strained his eyes in the direction from which the reports had come, but it was like trying to see through a blanket. He leaped upon the rail and balanced himself there, to get greater elevation; his pipe, striking a rope, was knocked from his mouth. He lunged for it; a short, hoarse cry came from his lips as he realized he had reached too far and had lost his balance. The cry was pinched off short as the blood-warm waters of the Caribbean Sea closed over his head.

Did you guess that this character has fallen into the sea? You can correctly infer that he has fallen overboard a ship because ropes and rails are common items on a ship and because the narrator describes the warm water closing over his head.

In this chapter, you will learn how to make **inferences** and **conclusions**. These skills are important for improving your understanding of what you read.

- **Inferences** are made when you read text and make an educated guess about what is happening in the story based on what is actually written, what is hinted at, and your past experience and knowledge. Inferences are made when you "read between the lines."

- **Conclusions** are general statements you can make and support with details from a text. If you read a story describing a sport where players use a bat to hit a ball and then run around bases, you can likely conclude that the sport is baseball.

INFERENCES

Making **inferences** is reading a passage carefully and then making connections among all the pieces of information. As a reader, you also have to notice what is implied or hinted at and use your prior knowledge to fill in any gaps. Being able to make inferences is one of the most important skills a reader can develop.

Read the following passage in which the topic is not stated but must be inferred by the reader. Notice how the details that provide the clues in the paragraph help you make an inference.

Now that you've built up your arm and leg strength, you are ready to go. Before you begin, you need to remember that the sport requires more than a board and water. First, you need a great deal of balance. The waves are always changing and moving. The rider's feet must be positioned and repositioned on the board to avoid falling. Second, you need good vision. It is important to observe how your wave is changing and make adjustments. You also need to watch out for other people in the water. Third, you need patience. A lot of the time, you will just be sitting on your board and floating in the water while waiting for the perfect wave. Even when that wave arrives, don't be surprised when you fall off. It takes some time to get the right combination of movements together to catch the perfect wave. When that wave comes, you'll be ready for an awesome experience!

Did you infer that the topic of this passage is surfing? The following details provide clues.

Direct statements in the text:

- "First . . . a great deal of balance."

- "a board and water"

Clues that depend on connections and prior knowledge:

- "catch the perfect wave"; a phrase you have probably heard before
- water and waves mentioned; points to the ocean, not a lake or river
- "sitting on your board and floating in the water while waiting for the perfect wave"; describes what you have seen surfers doing

You could also draw other inferences about the selection. For example, you could infer that surfing is a challenging sport. The passage also suggests that surfing requires lots of practice.

Now reread the selection. Think of two other inferences you could make based on the passage. Then write your inferences on the spaces provided.

Inference_____

_____

Inference_____

_____

Look at the following newspaper ad and answer the questions that follow it.

Want Ad

Cheerful person to work at Medical City Minneapolis Hospital. Some experience selling helpful, but not necessary. You will help brighten our patients' days. Uniform provided. Apply at Flower Power, 7777 Forest Lane, Minneapolis, MN.

---

1. The person who takes this job will probably work as a
   A. nurse.   B. receptionist.   C. salesperson.   D. custodian.

2. What two details tell you what kind of job this is?

You should be able to infer that the job opening is for a salesperson at a flower shop. Information concerning selling and the mention of Flower Power are the basis for the inference. "You will help brighten our patients' days" gives the clue that you will be doing something nice for the patients. The mention of the hospital and the uniform apply equally well to the jobs of nurse, receptionist, and custodian.

Practice 1: Inferences

Read the following passage. Choose the best inference or generalization for each question.

Excerpt from *The Adventures of Huckleberry Finn* by Mark Twain

At first I hated the school, but by-and-by I got so I could stand it. Whenever I got uncommon tired I played hookey, and the hiding [whipping] I got next day done me good and cheered me up. So the longer I went to school the easier it got to be. I was getting sort of used to the widow's ways, too, and they warn't so raspy on me. Living in a house, and sleeping in a bed, pulled on me pretty tight, mostly, but before the cold weather I used to slide out and sleep in the woods, sometimes, and so that was a rest to me. I like the old ways best, but I was getting so I liked the new ones, too, a little bit. The widow said I was coming along slow but sure, and doing very satisfactory. She said she warn't ashamed of me.

1. Based on the passage, we can infer that

    A.   the narrator likes going to school.

    B.   the narrator is struggling with his new life.

    C.   the widow is wealthy.

    D.   the narrator enjoys sleeping in a bed.

2. The passage suggests that the narrator is

    A.   a good student.

    B.   not used to living indoors.

    C.   angry.

    D.   trying to earn a living.

3. Which of the following events has likely happened?

    A.   The narrator has run away from home.

    B.   The narrator has gone to live in a new place.

    C.   The widow has made life easy for the narrator.

    D.   A fire has burned the narrator's house down.

4. Which of the following inferences can be made based on the passage?

    A.   The widow is strict but cares about the narrator.

    B.   The narrator once lived in a treehouse.

    C.   The widow is a retired school teacher.

    D.   The narrator will become a good student.

Practice 2:   More Inferences

Newspapers and Magazines. Read 2–3 articles or stories from newspapers or magazines. What inferences can you make from the information given? Support your inferences with facts or details from the selections. Share your findings with other students.

CONCLUSIONS

Skilled readers are always drawing **conclusions**. To reach a conclusion, you use two sources of information; you combine the written text with what you already know. Then you can come up with a statement about the topic. The statement or conclusion must be based on both sources of information. It must also reasonably and logically follow the information. Drawing conclusions helps you find connections between ideas and events and helps you better understand what you are reading.

Read the following passage. Check the most logical conclusion you can draw from this passage.

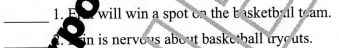

> Erin had been practicing for basketball tryouts. She had her older brother play with her every afternoon for weeks. She had dreams about playing basketball. On the morning of tryouts, her stomach began to ache.

> _____ 1. Erin will win a spot on the basketball team.

> _____ 2. Erin is nervous about basketball tryouts.

> _____ 3. Erin works hard for what she wants.

Here is an explanation of the answers:

Statement (**1**) is not a logical conclusion but is a prediction. Erin is not guaranteed to make the team. There could be a lot of competition for only a few spots, or Erin could not be very good at the game.

Statement (**2**) is a logical conclusion. We can conclude Erin is nervous about tryouts since she has practiced for long hours and has a stomach ache in the morning.

Statement (**3**) is a not a logical conclusion. The passage only mentions basketball. There is no evidence that shows she works hard at everything she wants.

When you read a passage with the purpose of drawing a conclusion, you need to read very carefully, paying special attention to the facts and details. Whatever conclusion you come to has to be supported by information from the paragraph.

To practice, read the following paragraph, and then answer the question.

Excerpt from "The Widow and the Parrot" by Virginia Woolf

Mrs. Gage, as I have already said, was lame in her right leg. At the best of times she walked slowly, and now, what with her disappointment and the mud on the bank, her progress was very slow indeed. As she plodded along, the day grew darker and darker, until it was as much as she could do to keep on the raised path by the river side. You might have heard her grumbling as she walked and complaining of her crafty brother Joseph, who had put her to all this trouble. "Express," she said, "to plague me. He was always a cruel little boy when we were children," she went on. "…I make no doubt that he's all aflame at this very moment in fire, but what's the comfort of that to me?" she asked, and indeed it was very little comfort, for she ran slap into a great cow which was coming along the bank, and rolled over and over in the mud.

Based on this paragraph, we can conclude that Mrs. Gage was—

A. very close to her brother.

B. an elderly woman, grouchy and lame.

C. a pleasant, able woman.

D. a farmer's wife who knew about cows.

After reading the paragraph carefully, you must choose the best conclusion. This requires you to look only at the responses that contain stated information from the paragraph. If the response cannot be supported by facts or details from the paragraph, then it would not be a correct conclusion.

Following this process, you would not choose A. Instead of being close to her brother, the author said Mrs. Gage complained about her brother and called him cruel. You would not choose C as the correct conclusion because the passage mentioned that she was grumbling. Choice D is not correct because although the passage mentioned a cow, we have no clues about Mrs. Gage's relationship to the cow. Therefore, the best answer is B. The facts and details about Mrs. Gage's lame right leg, her disappointment, and her grumbling and complaining all support the conclusion that she is grouchy and lame.

Practice 3:   Conclusions

Read the following passages. Check only the valid conclusions from the choices given after each passage. Then, support your answer with evidence.

What Kills Birds?

There are many ways birds can die, but countless die each year from human-related causes. Hunters kill 121 million birds each year. An estimated 50 to 100 million birds are killed each year by cars and trucks on America's highways. Agricultural pesticides poison 67 million birds per year. Dr. Daniel Klem conducted a 20-year study that looked at bird collisions with windows. He found that one billion birds are killed each year by flying into glass windows.

Which of the following is a valid conclusion?

_____ 1. Birds are killed most often by cars and trucks.

_____ 2. Glass windows are more dangerous to birds than any other human factor.

Evidence for your choice:

_____

_____

Chapter 3

Paying for the Win

Baseball teams spend a lot of money to recruit the best players. These teams hope spending top dollar for the best players will be the key to a winning season. The New York Yankees have high hopes for Alex Rodriguez. The club paid him $22 million in 2004, making him baseball's highest-paid player. In 2000, the L.A. Dodgers spent $15 million dollars for Kevin Brown but came in second place in their division. The Chicago White Sox spent $10 million for Albert Belle in 1997, a season in which they lost more games than they won. Several other teams over the past 13 years have had the highest-paid players in the league but have failed to win a championship.

Which of the following is a valid conclusion?

_____ 3. Having the highest-paid players does not guarantee success.

_____ 4. Alex Rodriguez will guarantee the Yankees a successful season.

Evidence for your choice:

_____

_____

Picking a Pet

The decision to get a family pet is usually surrounded by happy emotions. You see an animal in a shop window, fall in love, and bring it home. However, this kind of spur-of-the moment decision may end up being a disaster. It is important to investigate different types of animals before making a decision. It's also a good idea to arrange visits with the pet to see how you interact. All animals need attention, some more than others, so you should also consider how much time you have to spend with your pet.

Which is a valid conclusion?

_____ 5. Choosing a family pet is an important decision that needs careful consideration.

_____ 6. You should choose a pet that you love.

Evidence for your choice:

_____

_____

Excerpt from "The Monkey's Paw" by W. W. Jacobs

At the foot of the stairs the match went out, and he paused to strike another, and at the same moment a knock, so quiet and stealthy as to be scarcely audible, sounded on the front door.

The matches fell from his hand. He stood motionless, his breath suspended until the knock was repeated. Then he turned and fled swiftly back to his room, and closed the door behind him. A third knock sounded through the house.

"What's that?" cried the old woman, starting up.

"A rat," said the old man, in shaking tones—"a rat. It passed me on the stairs."

His wife sat up in bed listening. A loud knock resounded through the house.

"It's Herbert!" she screamed. "It's Herbert!"

She ran to the door, but her husband was before her, and catching her by the arm, held her tightly.

"What are you going to do?" he whispered hoarsely.

"It's my boy; it's Herbert!" she cried, struggling mechanically. "I forgot it was two miles away. What are you holding me for? Let go. I must open the door."

"For God's sake, don't let it in," cried the old man trembling.

Which of the following is a valid conclusion?

_____ 7. The old man is excited.

_____ 8. The old man is afraid.

Evidence for your choice:

_____

_____

Practice 4: More Conclusions

Newspapers and Magazines. Read 2 – 3 articles and stories from newspapers, magazines, or the Internet. What conclusions can you make from the information? Write down the facts or details that support your conclusions. Share your findings with other students. Is there agreement about the conclusions?

CHAPTER 3 SUMMARY

- An **inference** is an educated guess based on clues and information in a text. It is also based on your prior knowledge and life experiences.
- Making valid inferences from your reading requires practice and attention to detail.
- A **conclusion** is a general statement you can make based on the entire text.
- Drawing conclusions brings **clarity** and **purpose** to your reading.

CHAPTER 3 REVIEW

Read the following passages. Then answer the questions after each one.

Excerpt from "The Most Dangerous Game" by Richard Connell

"The place has a reputation — a bad one." [said Whitney.]

"Cannibals?" suggested Rainsford.

"Hardly. Even cannibals wouldn't live in such a God-forsaken place. But it's gotten into sailor lore, somehow. Didn't you notice that the crew's nerves seemed a bit jumpy today?"

"They were a bit strange, now you mention it. Even Captain Nielsen —"

"Yes, even that tough-minded old Swede, who'd go up to the devil himself and ask him for a light. Those fishy blue eyes held a look I never saw there before. All I could get out of him was 'This place has an evil name among seafaring men, sir.' Then he said to me, very gravely, 'Don't you feel anything?' — as if the air about us was actually poisonous. Now, you mustn't laugh when I tell you this — I did feel something like a sudden chill.

"There was no breeze. The sea was as flat as a plate glass window. We were drawing near the island then. What I felt was a — a mental chill; a sort of sudden dread."

"Pure imagination," said Rainsford. "One superstitious sailor can taint the whole ship's company with his fear."

"Maybe. But sometimes I think sailors have an extra sense that tells them when they are in danger. Sometimes I think evil is a tangible thing — with wave lengths, just as sound and light have. An evil place can, so to speak, broadcast vibrations of evil. Anyhow, I'm glad we're getting out of this zone. Well, I think I'll turn in now, Rainsford."

1. What inferences can you make about what might happen on the island?

   A. The sailors will take a break.

   B. Rainsford will make a remarkable discovery.

   C. Something horrible and evil will happen.

   D. They will stop to gather supplies.

2. What details from the passage helped you make your inference?

_____

_____

_____

3. What inference about sailors do Whitney and Rainsford (the two speakers) make?

   A. Sailors are skilled at navigating.   C. Sailors like to tell stories.

   B. Sailors are superstitious.   D. Sailors are evil.

4. In the last paragraph, what is Whitney, the speaker, implying about evil?

   A. Evil is all around us.   C. Evil is created by imagination.

   B. Evil is within each of us.   D. Evil will never win over good.

5. What conclusion has Rainsford come to when he says, "pure imagination?"

   A. There is nothing to fear on the island.   C. The island is imaginary.

   B. Imagination is pure entertainment.   D. The sailors are imaginary.

"To My Dear and Loving Husband"
by Anne Bradstreet

If ever two were one, then surely we.
If ever man were loved by wife, then thee;
If ever wife was happy in a man,
Compare with me, ye women, if you can.
I prize thy love more than whole mines of gold
Or all the riches that the East doth hold.
My love is such that rivers cannot quench,
Nor ought but love from thee, give recompense.
Thy love is such I can no way repay,
The heavens reward thee manifold, I pray.
Then while we live, in love let's so persevere
That when we live no more, we may live ever.

6. What can the reader infer from the last line of the poem?

   A. The narrator and her husband are about to die.

   B. The narrator wants to live forever.

   C. The narrator and her husband's love will live no more.

   D. The narrator and her husband's love will live on, even after death.

7. Which of the following inferences can you make from this poem?

   A. The narrator's love is like a rushing river.

   B. The narrator values her love for her husband.

   C. The narrator's husband does not repay her love.

   D. The narrator's love is not lasting.

8. Which lines from the poem help support this inference?

   _____

   _____

Chapter 3

Out of Luck, Out of Time

When Scott and Manuel started this whole scheme, they had no idea things would get so bad. It was due in part to poor planning, but bad luck had a lot to do with it. It seemed that the project was doomed from the beginning. Now they were in over their heads and didn't see any hope of things getting better. What were they going to do now? Confess was one option, but that choice didn't interest them much. They could always place the blame on someone else, maybe Louisa and her whole annoying group. That didn't really seem like the best choice either. They liked making mischief, but didn't necessarily want to be cruel. It seemed their choices were limited. Mom always said that honesty was the best policy. The problem is that honesty right now could really get them in trouble. They couldn't afford to spoil their records right now. It would make all their hard work a waste, not to mention the disappointment. Why didn't they listen all those times Mom told them to slow down and think about the consequences?

9. What inference can you make about what Scott and Manuel have done?

   A. They are always getting into trouble.   C. They don't think things through.

   B. They enjoy teasing girls.   D. They are liars.

10. Which of the following conclusions about Scott and Manuel can you make from the passage?

   A. They have just accomplished something great.

   B. They are proud of what they've done.

   C. They have planned something cruel.

   D. They have made a serious mistake.

Excerpt from *Walden* by Henry David Thoreau

As for clothing, to come at once to the practical part of the question, perhaps we are led oftener by the love of novelty and a regard for the opinions of men, in procuring it, than by true utility. Let him who has work to do recollect that the object of clothing is, first, to retain the vital heat, and secondly, in this state of society, to cover nakedness, and he may judge how much of any necessary or important work may be accomplished without adding to his wardrobe.

11. Based on the passage, which of the following is a valid conclusion than can be reached?

   A. Thoreau believes that work clothing should be chosen for warmth and practicality.

   B. Thoreau believes that clothing should always be chosen strictly on the basis of practical reasons, without regard to fashion.

   C. Thoreau believes that novel, or unusual, clothing will always draw attention and therefore is not suitable for work wear.

   D. Thoreau believes that the main question about clothing should always be "How much clothing is necessary to cover nakedness?"

12. **Open-ended Response.** Use your own paper to write your response.

One inference that can be made from this passage is that probably Thoreau doesn't give much thought to the clothes he puts on everyday. Explain which details from the passage would support that inference.

America's Youth Is Being Super Sized

Would you like that super sized? Teenagers in America are hearing this question all too often. All too often, they are answering, "Yes." That answer could mean saying yes to serious health problems such as heart disease, stroke, diabetes, cancer, high blood pressure, and Type 2 diabetes—all health problems that increase with obesity. Over the past 20 years, the percentage of obese children aged 6 to 19 has tripled. There are now about nine million excessively overweight children in America.

What's causing this increase in obesity? Health experts say junk foods and huge portion sizes. Pizza and kid's meals are cheap and easy alternatives to home-cooked meals. In a teenager's busy life of soccer practice and homework, this is the choice for dinner many nights of the week. The problem is most fast foods are too high in calories, fat, and artery-clogging cholesterol to eat them that often. The trend toward larger portions, or super sizing, is also contributing to the big fat problem. In 1957, the average fast-food burger weighed about one ounce. Today, the average burger weighs six ounces.

Some companies have chosen to shape up their menus in an effort to reduce the obesity problem. Experts say that such changes are good, but more needs to be done. They say we need to hold the fast-food industry accountable for its marketing of unhealthy options to children.

The government is also making an effort. The U.S. Department of Agriculture (USDA) is changing its nutrition guidelines to make it easier for people to use. The USDA is also offering healthier choices in public schools. This year, the USDA bought more than 973 million pounds of fruits and vegetables for school meals, 22% more than in 2002.

So teens can go ahead and supersize that salad and slice of watermelon!

13. From the information presented, what conclusion can we make about fast food?

_____

_____

_____

14. From the information in the article, what conclusion can you make about the rate of obesity in children during the next ten years?

_____

_____

_____

15. What inference might the reader make about fast-food companies?

_____

_____

_____

From the Introduction to *Hero Tales of American History*
by Theodore Roosevelt and Henry Cabot Lodge

It is a good thing for all Americans, and it is an especially good thing for young Americans, to remember the men who have given their lives in war and peace to the service of their fellow-countrymen, and to keep in mind the feats of daring and personal prowess done in time past by some of the many champions of the nation in the various crises of her history. Thrift, industry, obedience to law, and intellectual cultivation are essential qualities in the makeup of any successful people; but no people can be really great unless they possess also the heroic virtues which are as needful in time of peace as in time of war, and as important in civil as in military life.

16. **Open-ended Response.** Use your own paper to write your response.

Predict how the authors would recommend we celebrate Veteran's Day. Use details from the passage to support your prediction.

They Keep Listening

Some scientists are listening to the stars. They belong to an organization called SETI, Search for Extraterrestrial Intelligence, whose mission is to explore life in the universe. Most SETI enthusiasts believe it is just a matter of time before we make contact with aliens. Their belief is based on numbers. The Milky Way has an estimated 400 billion stars, including the Sun. SETI scientists believe that many of these stars have life-sustaining planets orbiting them.

The first SETI search began in the Allegheny Mountains of West Virginia. In 1960, Dr. Frank D. Drake, a young scientist at the National Radio Astronomy Observatory there, used an 85-foot antenna to listen for alien transmissions around a few stars. Since then, SETI's main strategy has been to use increasingly immense radio telescopes to keep listening. One such telescope is in Arecibo, Puerto Rico. The dish antenna at Arecibo is 1,000 feet wide, making it the world's largest radio telescope. The Arecibo Observatory recently celebrated its fortieth birthday and continues to be used by SETI scientists searching for alien life. The scientists focus their search on close stars, since signals from their inhabited planets would be strongest. They also look at stars similar to the sun, the only star known to support life. Lastly, they search older stars, since they assume advanced life takes time to evolve.

SETI has found no extraterrestrials so far, but it has continued to probe the heavens regularly. Despite long hours and decades of failure, the scientists keep their ears open, waiting for their proof.

17. Which conclusion can the reader make about SETI scientists?

   A. They are dedicated to their mission.

   B. They get frustrated easily.

   C. Success is important to them.

   D. They believe aliens have visited us.

18. Based on evidence from the article, what conclusion can you draw about the discovery of alien life?

   A. Only stars close by will have life.

   B. Alien life will be discovered in our lifetime.

   C. Life may be found in a solar system similar to ours.

   D. Alien life will be discovered in the Milky Way.

Excerpt from *The Call of The Wild* by Jack London

It was at Circle City, ere the year was out, that Pete's apprehensions were realized. "Black" Burton, a man evil-tempered and malicious, had been picking a quarrel with a tenderfoot at the bar, when Thornton stepped good-naturedly between. Buck, as was his custom, was lying in a corner, head on paws, watching his master's every action. Burton struck out, without warning, straight from the shoulder. Thornton was sent spinning, and saved himself from falling only by clutching the rail of the bar.

Those who were looking on heard what was neither bark nor yelp, but something which is best described as a roar, and they saw Buck's body rise up in the air as he left the floor for Burton's throat. The man saved his life by instinctively throwing out his arm, but was hurled backward to the floor with Buck on top of him. Buck loosed his teeth from the flesh of the arm and drove in again for the throat. This time the man succeeded only in partly blocking, and his throat was torn open. Then the crowd was upon Buck, and he was driven off; but while a surgeon checked the bleeding, he prowled up and down, growling furiously, attempting to rush in, and being forced back by an array of hostile clubs. A "miners' meeting," called on the spot, decided that the dog had sufficient provocation, and Buck was discharged. But his reputation was made, and from that day his name spread through every camp in Alaska.

19. Which is the correct inference about what is happening in the passage?

   A. The miners are watching a boxing match.

   B. A man has attacked Buck.

   C. Buck has attacked a man to defend his owner.

   D. Buck has gone wild.

20. What clues led you to that inference?

_____

_____

21. What inference can you make about how miners will react to Buck?

   A. They will greet him with pats on the head.

   B. They will fear him.

   C. They will try to capture him.

   D. They will beat him with clubs.

22. Support your inference with information from the passage.

_____

_____

_____

23. What conclusion can you draw about Buck's character?

   A. He is loyal, observant, and strong.

   B. He is mean, dangerous, and deadly.

   C. He is wild and weak.

   D. He is rapid and confused.

24. What details from the passage support your conclusion?

_____

_____

_____

The Day They Found Out

    When Sandra walked into the room, she knew instantly that something was wrong. Things didn't sound right; it was too quiet. Robert and his crowd weren't horsing around as usual. In fact, nothing was as usual. Everyone was sitting quietly at the desks. Normally, it took at least five minutes for everyone to settle down. That was one of the great things about math class; she got a chance to catch up on all the latest gossip. Mr. Martin was always so cool about letting them relax into their assignments for the day, but today was different. Mr. Martin had that look on his face, the one that said, today is not the day to mess with me. Sandra was familiar with that face. Her mother wore it often, especially on days when she had worked late.

25. What conclusion can you draw about this story? Use evidence from the passage to support your conclusion.

_____

_____

_____

_____

26. Using the information already given, what conclusions can you make about Sandra?

_____

_____

_____

Chapter 4
Fact and Opinion

This chapter covers Minnesota Reading Standard(s):

I.C.11	Students will distinguish fact from opinion in two selections and on the same topic and give evidence.

Imagine that you and your friend are leaving a school assembly. During the assembly, the Cue-less Comedy Troupe had demonstrated the hilarious art of improvisational theater. Your friend Callie is still laughing.

"That was the funniest assembly we've ever had!" Callie says when she catches her breath.

"Well, you know, The Cue-less won the Best-Theater-Without-a-Script Award for St. Cloud last year," you offer. "I read it in the newspaper yesterday."

Which of you is expressing an opinion? Which one is voicing a fact?

Your friend has expressed an **opinion**. She felt that the assembly was funnier than any other assembly. She made a statement of personal feeling that cannot be proven. On the other hand, you expressed a **fact**. A fact is a true statement. It can be proven by research. If you researched the records of the "Best-Theater-Without-a-Script" Award, you would find Cue-less Comedy Troupe listed among the winners (if this story were not imaginary!).

Authors express both opinions and facts. If an author writes mostly opinion, the **author's perspective** is **biased**. If mostly facts are presented, the author's perspective is **objective**.

In this chapter, you will learn to distinguish between facts and opinions. You will also compare the presentation of facts and opinions in paired passages in the chapter review.

FINDING FACTS AND OPINIONS

Facts, as you read above, are statements of information. That information can be proven through observation or research. **Opinions** express a personal viewpoint or belief about a person, place, event, or idea. Being able to distinguish a fact from an opinion is an important reading skill. Let's look at some facts and opinions.

Fact and Opinion

1a. Fact: American colleges often profit from football, both in money and in fame.

1b. Opinion: Football is exciting to watch and fun to play.

2a. Fact: Texas Instruments made the first electronic handheld calculator.

2b. Opinion: Texas Instruments calculators make math easier and more enjoyable.

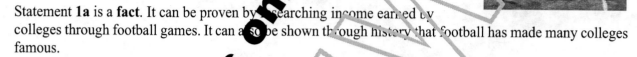

Statement **1a** is a **fact**. It can be proven by researching income earned by colleges through football games. It can also be shown through history that football has made many colleges famous.

Statement **1b** about the excitement and fun of football is an **opinion**. It may be true for many people, but not everyone. Many people may not enjoy watching or playing football at all.

Statement **2a** about Texas Instruments is a **fact**. It can be proven through historical records that the first calculator was made by "TI."

On the other hand, statement **2b** is clearly an **opinion** since the phrase "easier and more enjoyable" describes one person's experience. It does not apply to everyone.

Tips for Identifying Facts and Opinions

1. **Facts state information** based on observation, statistics, or research.

2. **Opinions express a personal viewpoint** or belief about a person, place, event, or idea.

   Hint 1: Opinions contain adjectives like *best*, *worst*, *favorite*, *dishonest*, *fun*, and so on.

   Hint 2: Opinions sometimes include phrases such as *"you should," "I think," "my view," "my opinion,"* and so on.

Practice 1: Fact or Opinion

A. Read the following paragraph. See if you can distinguish the factual statements from those that are opinions. On the spaces that follow the passage, write the numbers of the sentences that are fact and the ones that are opinion.

1) You don't have to play a strenuous sport to get your exercise. **2)** You don't have to belong to an expensive gym or buy expensive clothing or equipment, either. **3)** Research has shown that regular walking is as good for you as most other exercises. **4)** A short brisk walk around the neighborhood every day is also a lot of fun. **5)** A good time to take walks is after school. **6)** Most school days involve too much sitting still. **7)** Walking exercises the muscles and increases oxygen in the blood and lungs. **8)** Walking and talking with a friend is much better than visiting over the phone. **9)** In general, walking is a great way to end a long school day!

Facts: _____   Opinions: _____

B. For the following statements, write *F* next to facts and *O* next to opinions. Be able to support your responses.

1. _____ Bicycling is the best sport for building strong lungs.

2. _____ The Mississippi River flows past the city of Winona.

3. _____ Vegetables are delicious and nutritious.

4. _____ The food pyramid advises including vegetables in the diet every day.

5. _____ Nolan Ryan was the greatest pitcher in the history of baseball.

6. _____ Tom Landry of the Dallas Cowboys had the third most NFL wins ever.

7. _____ I think that middle school is more fun than elementary school.

8. _____ You should take part in as many school activities as possible.

9. _____ Watching television is a bad habit.

10. _____ Minnesota has more than 12,000 lakes.

11. _____ The new CD by White Stripes is their best one yet.

12. _____ Eating in restaurants can be more expensive than eating at home.

13. _____ Dozens of Australian horsemen helped usher in the 2000 Olympics.

14. _____ Swim meets are the most exciting part of summer.

15. _____ Tonka trucks are named after the town of Minnetonka where they are still manufactured.

Practice 2: Reading for Facts and Opinions

Use your own paper to write your response.

For the following passage, clearly explain why statements 1, 3, 4, and 5 are facts and statements 2, 6, 7, 8, 9, and 10 are opinions. Use details from the passage to give reasons for your responses.

A Formal Night Out

(1) I don't often go to places that require formal attire. (2) Jeans are much more comfortable. (3) But tonight my dad and I are in suits, and my mom is in her best dress. (4) We are at the metrodome to listen to the Minnesota Orchestra. (5) I usually spend Friday nights with my friends at the school football game. (6) But for a couple of Friday nights each year, somehow, this concert hall is just as much fun. (7) The audience is so

proper that they almost appear snobbish. (8) But soon the grand array of musicians on the stage fills the hall with magnificent sound. (9) Then the audience becomes the warmest, most inspired group of people you can imagine. (10) Everyone should experience the symphony at least a few times in their lives.

Practice 3: Creating Facts and Opinions

Think of two persons, places, things, or ideas on your own or with a partner. Then write a statement of fact and a statement of opinion about each one. Review your statements with a teacher or other students. Revise them based on the feedback you get.

Practice 4: Finding Facts and Opinions

Find five facts and five opinions in newspaper articles, magazine articles, or Internet articles. Underline them, and then share them with your instructor or classmates. Research the facts in one of the articles to make sure they are true. Present this research to the class.

Practice 5: Identifying Fact and Opinion

A. Read the passage below. Answer the questions that follow it.

Winter Guests of Aransas

The whooping crane is one of the most beautiful migrating birds in the world. Tall and stately, with snowy white wings spanning seven feet, the crane is a treasure of the state of Texas. It was not always so. The "whooper" almost became extinct in the early part of the century. Thanks to careful conservation efforts of Canada and the United States, the cranes continue to seek out their winter home each year in the South. In October, the cranes fly 2,400 miles from northern Canada to the coast of Texas. There, they live in the Aransas National Wildlife Refuge until spring. Their numbers are increasing, but they still need protection and care from humans. One of the most important ways to help the whooping crane is to prevent pollution in the Gulf of Mexico. The Gulf is where the cranes find much of their food. People can visit the wildlife refuge in Aransas and view these rare and wonderful creatures during the months of October through April.

1. Which one of the following statements is a *fact* expressed in the passage?

   A.   Whooping cranes are rare and wonderful creatures.

   B.   Cranes are a valuable state treasure.

   C.   Cranes find most of their food in the waters of the Gulf of Mexico.

   D.   Cranes are one of the most beautiful birds in the world.

2. Which one of the following statements is an *opinion* expressed in the passage?

    A.   Whooping cranes were once almost extinct.

    B.   Whooping cranes live in a refuge in Aransas, Texas, during the winter.

    C.   The whooping cranes fly 2,400 miles every autumn.

    D.   The whooping crane is a stately bird.

B. Read the ad below. Then on a separate sheet of paper, write three statements from the ad that are facts. Next, write three statements that are opinion. Determine whether there are more *statements of fact* or more *statements of opinion* in this ad.

High School Rings: Your Badge of Success!

You've worked hard for four years. You deserve a trophy. Now you get to wear one!

High school rings are a tradition in American education.
Now, you are one of the privileged few who can claim this prized emblem.

The high school ring is the key to the doors of your future!
The high school ring is your badge of honor!

Show your individual style by choosing from our great selection of fine "Jewelry of Tribute."

Girls' rings
The *Scholar* (stainless steel) – $163
The *Brilliance* (silver) – $339
The *Executive* (yellow gold) – $549

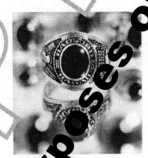

Boys' rings

The *Flagship* (stainless steel) – $198
The *CEO* (silver) – $449
The *Triumph* (yellow gold) – $654

Lifetime Warranty: We'll repair any poor workmanship or materials.
Guaranteed satisfaction: You'll love our product.
Guaranteed safe shipment: If you buy it, we'll deliver it.
Guaranteed easy payments: Your parents will be *happy* with these monthly payments.

All sales are final.
Remember, high school students always buy class rings!

CHAPTER 4 SUMMARY

- A **fact** is a statement that can be proven by observation or research.
- **Factual passages** present a **balanced** or **objective** perspective on a topic.
- An **opinion** is a statement of person belief or viewpoint.
- **Opinionated passages** present a **biased** or **subjective** perspective on a topic.

CHAPTER 4 REVIEW

A. For each of the following statements, write *F* if it expresses a fact or *O* if it expresses an opinion.

_____ 1. The beach is a better place for vacation than the mountains.

_____ 2. It doesn't matter where you buy your clothes, as long as you buy them from the "cool" stores.

_____ 3. The girls got more points in volleyball today than the boys did.

_____ 4. Parents should let 14-year-olds go to any movie they want to see.

_____ 5. Who needs libraries when you have the Internet?

_____ 6. The trend towards home-schooling in America is growing stronger every year.

_____ 7. Skateboarding improves fitness, teaches coordination, and is an exciting sport.

_____ 8. Jay McLean was excellent in the role of Paul Bunyan in the class skit.

B. Read the following passage. For each of the numbered sentences, write *F* if the sentence is a fact, and write *O* if the sentence is an opinion.

Lance Armstrong

(9) When Lance Armstrong was a teenager in Plano, Texas, he used to ride his bike on Saturdays. (10) But Lance's rides were extraordinary. (11) He often cycled from Plano, near Dallas, to the border of Oklahoma. (12) Then, as if Texas were not big enough, after high school Lance took his bike overseas. (13) Soon, he was winning cycling races all over Europe. (14) Before Lance began to compete in Europe, cycling had always been a European sport. (15) American cycling teams had nothing like the talent of the Europeans. (16) But now, Americans are very proud of their winning cycling team. (17) As of 2004, the team's leader, Armstrong, has won a record six Tour de France races. (18) The Tour de France is the most exciting event in sports. (19) Cyclists race for almost 2,000 miles in all kinds of landscapes and weather. (20) Each day, the teams race one section

of the whole race. (21) Whoever wins the section of the race gets to wear a yellow jersey (over shirt). (22) That jersey is starting to look like the uniform of the U.S. cycling team!

| 9. ____ | 11. ____ | 13. ____ | 15. ____ | 17. ____ | 19. ____ | 21. ____ |
| 10. ____ | 12. ____ | 14. ____ | 16. ____ | 18. ____ | 20. ____ | 22. ____ |

C. Read the following paired passages. Then, on your own paper, write whether each passage is objective or biased. If it is biased, what is the author's bias toward the subject in each passage? Give two examples from each of the passages to support your responses.

Uncommon Soldiers

Every year, hundreds of young Americans go into training for the U.S. military. And every year, over 300 of these "troops" are dogs: German shepherds and Dobermans. Dogs have been part of the military for decades. They have played important roles in most American wars. The location for training these special soldiers is the Lackland Air Force Base in San Antonio, Texas. It takes about 100 days to train the dogs to work in the military. After graduation, the dogs serve in all areas of the military: Army, Navy, Marines, and Special Forces. They serve at home and at war. Some are scout dogs. They sniff out explosives, booby-traps, and dangerous chemicals. Others are sentry dogs. They walk the battle line with their handlers to watch for enemies. Dogs are a definite part of national security.

Unsung Heroes

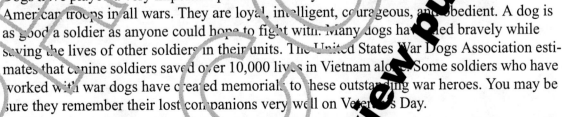

The cool, damp winds of November blow through the crowds along the Veterans' Day parade route. Flags fly and soldiers march, but all is not celebration. The skies are usually bleak. People's thoughts turn to lost heroes of past wars. They ponder the fact that they are safe and free today because of these fallen heroes. But how many Americans think, at this time, about dogs? Dogs have played a very important part in the safety of American troops in all wars. They are loyal, intelligent, courageous, and obedient. A dog is as good a soldier as anyone could hope to fight with. Many dogs have died bravely while saving the lives of other soldiers in their units. The United States War Dogs Association estimates that canine soldiers saved over 10,000 lives in Vietnam alone. Some soldiers who have worked with war dogs have created memorials to these outstanding war heroes. You may be sure they remember their lost companions very well on Veterans' Day.

D. More Author's Perspective: Objective or Biased. On the next page are two paired passages. As in the previous exercise, read each one carefully. Then, on your own paper, write whether each passage is objective or biased. If it is biased, what is the author's bias toward the subject in each passage? Give two examples from each of the passages to support your responses.

Fact and Opinion

Mangy Wolves and Little Lambs

Ranchers in Montana, Idaho, and Wyoming have lived as farmers for generations. Americans are fond of images of these cowboys and cowgirls rustling cattle and sheep through vast tracts of ranch land. Many Americans rely on the meat, produced by these ranchers, for nutritious and delicious meals. Yet, these symbols of the American West and providers of food for the country are facing a threat. For decades, there were no wolves in these states. But some people missed having wolves in the wild. In the 1990s, they transported sixty-six grey wolves from Alberta, Canada. These wolves were released in Idaho. They have now grown to over three hundred in population. Wolves live by hunting. A pasture full of sheep or grasslands full of cattle are attractive to them. When farmers lose livestock, they lose money. When farmers lose livestock, the price of those steak dinners that Americans enjoy goes up.

Princes of the Wilderness

Thousands of people from around the world come to Yellowstone National Park every year. They want to see a wilderness untouched by human hands. One of the favorite sights in the park is the noble wild beast, the gray wolf. Gray wolves are family animals. They are loyal to their pack. They support each other in survival. And all the members of a pack look after and play with the pups. The western United States was once home to hundreds of wolf packs. When

ranchers arrived in the 1800s, they cruelly wiped out the whole population of wolves. Wolves became an endangered species. Then, in the 1990s, supporters of wildlife started a plan to bring the wolves back. The project was one of the most successful ever tried on an endangered species. Today this magnificent animal freely roams its former homeland. A species almost destroyed by humans has been restored by human care.

Chapter 5
Evaluating Author's Evidence

This chapter covers Minnesota Reading Standard(s):

I.C.6	Students will evaluate the adequacy, accuracy, and appropriateness of the author's evidence in a persuasive text.
I.C.14	Students will critically read and evaluate to determine author's purpose, point of view, audience and message.

In this chapter, you will learn skills for recognizing an author's **viewpoint** and how the author presents the viewpoint. An author's viewpoint is the author's feelings about or attitude towards a topic. A viewpoint can be *biased* (one-sided) or it can be *objective* (neutral). Knowing an author's viewpoint allows you as a reader to judge the text for its effectiveness. You can determine if a text is effective by looking at the amount and the quality of **evidence** (forms of proof, examples, or other facts) the author presents in order to support his or her viewpoint.

This chapter will also look at how authors use **argument techniques** in presenting their viewpoints. These techniques can be used in a positive way by authors to present good ideas with persuasive evidence. They can also be used to manipulate or even mislead the reader, when presented with little or no evidence.

With practice, these questions will become an automatic part of your reading process. They help you to become an active, involved reader, who can gain as much from a text as it has to offer.

AUTHOR'S VIEWPOINT

Authors have a viewpoint, or a perspective, on each topic they write about. An author's **viewpoint** is the author's perspective or feeling about a topic. This viewpoint may be *objective* or based more on fact, or it can be *biased* or based more on opinion.

Evaluating Author's Evidence

Objective Viewpoint   Authors often write mainly *facts* about a topic, in order to inform or teach readers. When an author writes only to inform, then the author has an objective viewpoint. This viewpoint is common in *expository* writing. Objective writing informs the reader of facts about a topic. It does not state an opinion about the topic.

Biased Viewpoint   Authors also write to give their own *opinions* about a topic. When an author writes to express an opinion, the author has a biased viewpoint. A biased viewpoint is often used in *persuasive* writing. Persuasive writing urges the reader to agree with the author's opinion.

Following are two examples of objective writing and biased writing. Let's say your teacher has asked you to write about art and music in school. If you want to *inform* your reader about art and music in school, you would have an *objective point* of view. However, if you wanted to *give your opinion* about art and music in school, you would have a *biased* point of view.

Read the following two examples of different viewpoints on this topic.

Music in School: Objective Viewpoint

Art and music have been part of the American school system from its beginning. Today, the arts in public schools take many forms. American students may learn a lot about music. They may learn to sing, to play an instrument, and to read music. Students may also learn visual arts. These arts include painting, sculpting, and clay work. Some schools also offer classes in performing arts. The performing arts include acting and dancing. Music and visual art are the two most common arts subjects taught in schools. They are usually part of the everyday class schedule for elementary and middle school students.

Music in School: Biased Viewpoint

The arts are an important and fun part of education. Nothing adds a fresh outlook to a school day like an hour in the art room smoothing wet terra cotta clay with your hands into any shape you can dream of!

And singing or playing your heart out in the choir or band room gets rid of any tension and worry you might have about that math test. Some studies even show that learning music helps improve your skills in math! Losing music and art from our schools would be a tragedy. We need to support these valuable programs.

The first paragraph gives **facts** and information about the arts in school. It does not express an opinion about the topic. This is **objective** writing.

The second paragraph voices an **opinion** about the arts in school. The author gives examples of how the arts make a student's day more enjoyable. The author also mentions studies that support the author's ideas. The author uses the pronoun "we" to draw the reader into action to support art and music programs. The author's perspective in this paragraph is **biased**. It is biased toward keeping the arts in public schools.

For further practice, look at the statements below and decide for each one of them if the author's perspective is *objective*, to inform, or *biased*, to persuade. Then read the explanation of each that follows.

1. **According to the U.S. Fish and Wildlife Service, the California condor is an endangered species. In 2002, one condor chick was hatched in captivity for the first time in 18 years.**

2. **As responsible citizens, we must prevent the California condor, a national treasure, from disappearing from this earth.**

3. **Wolves are only trouble for ranchers. We should eliminate them through hunting and relocation.**

4. **The Louisiana Iris is celebrated in the spring of each year in Jean Lafitte, LA. Tours of swamps and gardens make it possible to get a good view of the flower in its habitats.**

Statements 1 and 4 state information and facts. They do not encourage one belief over another. These statements have an *objective* perspective.

Statements 2 and 3 urge the reader to take a certain action or adopt a certain belief. These statements have a *biased* perspective. You will notice that these biased statements use words like *must* and *should*. These key words often show that the author has a biased viewpoint about the topic and is encouraging the reader to feel the same.

Practice 1:   Biased Perspective

Read the following two passages. On your own piece of paper, write what you think the author's bias. Cite phrases or sentences from the passage to support your ideas.

Space Camp

Space camp is a valuable educational experience for middle school students. At the U.S. Space and Rocket Center in Huntsville, Alabama, students can attend a space camp for one week. There, they can experience moon-like gravity and learn about mission control operations. While having fun, students may also be preparing themselves for a good education and an exciting career. Several students who attended space camp in the last five years have been accepted into the top technical colleges in the country. When they graduate from these colleges as aeronautics engineers, they will have some of the best career opportunities in their field. The price of space camp seems like a good investment in the future!

Cast Call for Drama Club!

Middle schools offer several extra curricular activities for students. You can play basketball, soccer, badminton, and even chess before and after school. But not all middle schools have an active drama club. Being involved in drama helps young people to develop self confidence. They learn public speaking skills, develop good memories, learn about hard work, and make many friends. Just learning to overcome stage fright can be a life-changing event for a child. Middle school can be a time of uncertainty and shyness. Drama club can offer students a place to belong and a way to discover their talents. If any teachers are interested in starting drama clubs, they are needed to make a difference in kids' lives!

Biased Viewpoint: Indirect Bias

In the last exercise, you could probably see that the author's bias was quite obvious and clearly stated. However, authors do not always express their viewpoints directly. Instead, they often present their bias **indirectly**. This means that the author writes in a way that persuades the reader to adopt the author's bias but does not clearly state the bias. Indirect bias can be expressed by:

- Emphasizing information on one side of an issue
- Minimizing the importance of information on the other side of an issue
- Carefully choosing words that influence the reader to feel a certain way
- Choosing what information to include and what to ignore

All of the above techniques are effective in portraying an author's bias in an indirect way.

Read the following two passages. What is the author's bias? Can you detect how the author feels about the subject from the information given? Write down your answers, and then check them against the discussion which follows the passages.

Spring Fling Shopping

By February, the malls are brimming with new spring and summer clothes. Teenagers flock to the stores on weekends to see what new fashions they can find to add to their wardrobes. Tank tops, tee-shirts, sandals, and shorts, all in bright spring colors, decorate the store windows like flags at an Easter parade. It's all so difficult to decide on which ones to buy! Teens shop for many reasons. The pressure to dress well is one of the strongest forces in their lives. Clothing styles change every year. Furthermore, teens often grow from one year to the next, and last year's clothes do not fit anymore. Therefore, many young people, with parents in tow, head to the mall at the beginning of each season. It is time for the expensive but enjoyable process of finding new clothes and shoes. The price of these clothes, may not always reflect their quality. Clothes often look old within weeks of purchase. This results in clothing being donated to charities or thrown away, as families replace them with new styles, colors, and sizes. All this spending, growing, and discarding add up to a lively economy and long days at the mall for teens.

Mall Shops and Sweatshops

High school is full of motivating clubs and activities to take part in. Some high school clubs promote awareness of injustices in our world. One club of this kind is the anti-sweatshop club. An anti-sweatshop club educates students about where much of their clothing comes from. Students are often surprised to learn that a large percentage of the cool clothes they buy in the mall are made in sweatshops — in America and around the world. What is a sweatshop? It is a place where people work from morning until night under poor conditions for extremely low pay. It is a place where women work so much that they hardly see their children. And even then, they earn too little money to buy enough food for their families. Yet the clothes they make will earn millions for large companies. Newspaper reports about sweatshops have caused some students to want to make a difference. Through anti-sweatshop clubs, students learn about sweatshops and the companies that use them. Then they can write to these companies. A letter from a high school student has a lot of influence on companies that depend on young Americans to buy their products. A student can also write to the major department stores and ask which of their products come from sweatshops. Large department stores do not want to be seen as supporting sweatshops. Students in anti-sweatshop clubs believe in the power of teenagers to make a difference in their world.

The first passage contains mainly facts and information, but the viewpoint tends to be biased towards the fun and benefits of shopping. Malls are described in colorful, vibrant language, and people are described as happy and active. The author makes the point that the money spent supports a strong economy. This supports the viewpoint that shopping has beneficial effects.

The second passage is also full of facts and information. That information brings out a negative bias about the shopping situation. The author uses emotional images. The passage describes a mother too poor to feed her family while making clothes that make big companies rich. This idea will most likely influence a reader to feel that something is unjust in the clothing industry. The writer's opinion is not exactly stated in words, but it becomes clear to the reader through the choice of information given.

Tips for Recognizing an Author's Indirect Bias

Think carefully about the author's choice of words:

Objective: Students may study algebra when they are in 7th grade.

Indirect Bias: Students have the <u>opportunity</u> to study algebra as early as 7th grade.

Indirect Bias: Some students <u>have to</u> study algebra as early as 7th grade.

Study the supporting information the author chooses to include in the passage:

Objective: Many students enter medical school. Doctors earn large salaries. They also achieve a high level of education.

Indirect Bias: Many people enter medical school each year. A doctor's job is <u>very demanding</u>. Doctors can <u>suffer from</u> fatigue, anxiety, and depression.

Indirect Bias: Many people enter medical school each year. They are looking for the opportunity to <u>help people</u>. Doctors are able to make a <u>positive difference</u> in people's lives.

Look closely at how the author describes a situation or idea.

Objective: All the students in the class were busy with projects.

Indirect Bias: The business development classroom was a place of <u>activity</u>. The students worked cooperatively as <u>conversation</u> filled the air.

Indirect Bias: Students talked and moved around the <u>disordered</u> science lab while working on projects. The place seemed <u>chaotic</u> and <u>noisy</u>.

EVIDENCE: SUPPORTING A VIEWPOINT

Whether an author's perspective is biased or objective, it must be supported with evidence to be effective. Evidence can consist of examples, statistics, illustrations, or general facts. Evidence can also consist of good, sound logic. In any case, the more and better the evidence, the more an author's viewpoint will be considered valid.

Look at the following two paragraphs. The first one is not supported well with evidence. The second one includes plentiful evidence. As you read each paragraph, consider which one is more effective in influencing you to accept the writer's viewpoint.

The Marquis de Lafayette: Version 1

Marquis de Lafayette

The French nobleman and soldier, whose name is about three feet long, but who is commonly known as the Marquis de Lafayette, is a model of revolutionary spirit. He was a great soldier who played an important role in the American Revolution. He had a noble and honest character, which won him the respect of his troops and of his countrymen. Lafayette hated the oppressive rule of kings and fought for the rights of people. He is one of the most important figures in American history. Louisiana can be proud of having this great man associated with its history. Lafayette brought about dramatic changes in the government of France as well. Both the Americans and the French deeply mourned his death in 1834. He was one of the greatest champions of liberty that ever lived.

The Marquis de Lafayette: Version 2

The French nobleman and soldier whose name is about three feet long, but who is commonly known as the Marquis de Lafayette, is a model of revolutionary spirit. A wealthy orphan, he was only 16 years old when he heard that the United States had declared independence from England. From the moment he heard that news, he determined to be part of the American fight for independence. Though very young, he disobeyed orders and sailed to America to join the Continental Army. He was a great soldier who played an important role in the American Revolution. He fought with General George Washington, who also became his friend.

Lafayette returned to France to convince the French to support the Americans in their fight. Because of his efforts, many French officers and troops sailed to America and fought with the Americans against England. One of these officers was Admiral Rochambeau, who, along with Lafayette and another French officer, brought about the defeat of the British in Yorktown, one of the most important victories in the war. For this reason alone, Lafayette is an important figure in American history.

Lafayette had a noble and honest character, which won him the respect of his troops and of his countrymen. When he returned to France after the American Revolution, the French gave him a hero's welcome, calling him a "hero of two worlds." Lafayette hated the oppressive rule of kings and fought for the rights of people. While in France, he fought successfully for a more democratic form of government called the National Assembly. Lafayette brought about dramatic changes in the government of France. He wrote the "Declaration of the Rights of Man and of the Citizen" with some help from his friend, Thomas Jefferson. He then introduced this document to the General Assembly. The French Revolution against royalty followed soon after, leading to France's freedom from tyranny.

Louisiana can be proud of having this great man associated with its history. In 1803, Louisiana made a gift to Lafayette of a large portion of land. Lafayette also became an honorary citizen of the United States. Both the Americans and the French deeply mourned his death in 1834. He was one of the greatest champions of liberty that ever lived.

Authors may bring any point of view to their writing. Every writer has something to offer to the "conversation" which readers and authors take part in. However, the presentation of a viewpoint can be strong and convincing, or it can be weak and superficial. The difference lies in the evidence the author provides to support all points made in the writing.

ARGUMENT TECHNIQUES

Many of the written — and non-written — messages that we come across every day have something to convince us about. An author may want to convince a reader of the author's viewpoint. A business may want to convince a viewer or reader to buy a product. They both use **argument techniques** to do so.

Argument techniques in writing can be powerful tools for thoughtful writers to introduce readers to great ideas or new knowledge. They can also be powerful tools for manipulating readers and viewers. Argument techniques are used in both good persuasive writing and in advertising and propaganda. Learning to recognize argument techniques wherever they are used can help you analyze text.

With some exceptions, the same argument techniques are used both in **persuasive writing** (editorials, articles about social or political issues) and in **advertising**. They are just used differently in the two areas. Below are two lists of argument techniques and how they are applied to these two areas of writing. The first list applies to advertising. The second list applies to other persuasive writing such as editorials or essays. Study these lists, and try to see which techniques apply to the ads and passages in the rest of the chapter.

ARGUMENT TECHNIQUES IN ADVERTISING AND NONFICTION

APPEAL TO AUTHORITY

In advertising, the use of "**experts in the field**" is a common argument technique. Experts add authority and believability to the claims of advertisers.

> **Example:** A foot doctor, dressed in medical uniform, talks to a group of teens about the importance of supportive footwear. She says it will prevent serious pain from falling arches in the future. The purpose of this appeal to authority is to sell running shoes that claim to be supportive of feet.

In persuasive writing, the **appeal to authority** does not usually involve a professional in a uniform. But it may use the authority of a more experienced person or institution as an example of success. Referring to scientific studies is also a way of appealing to authority.

> **Example:** George Jones Middle School in Washington state began a tutoring program in reading, using middle school students as tutors for younger students. Since the beginning of the program, the reading scores of the students doing the tutoring have increased by 25%. It would not be difficult to try such a program in our school.

IN-CROWD APPEAL

In advertising, **in-crowd appeal** creates a kind of fantasy which encourages viewers to identify with an admired, envied group. The idea behind in-crowd appeal is that if the viewer buys the advertised product, he or she will be part of this "in crowd."

> **Example:** Young teens are shown at a festive party, very colorful and full of balloons and decorations. They are all wearing the latest fashions from an expensive teens' clothing store. They all look happy and as if they are having a fantastically wonderful time. The idea is that most teens would like to be part of that crowd, and it seems that if you buy those clothes, you will be.

BANDWAGON

No one likes to be left behind. In advertising, **bandwagon** is a technique in which the reader is made to feel that a great movement is beginning. When it is used in advertising, readers are made to believe they will be seen as idiots or outcasts if they do not join the movement.

> **Example:** "This is the age of the Internet. Which age do you belong to? Call our Internet service provider and get online...or get nowhere." The point of this slogan is that the reader should do what millions of people are doing, or they will "get nowhere." It does not give specific reasons why this is a good idea.

Non-fiction text does not usually try to cause anxiety in its readers about being left behind, the way advertising might. However, it may very effectively draw upon facts and statistics to show where trends are going and what the benefits of being part of those trends could be.

> **Example:** Employers today report that they are looking for workers who can think for themselves and who are creative in problem solving. Many high schools are encouraging creativity and "thinking outside the box" in order to prepare students for the better jobs the 21st century has to offer. Our school should consider being part of this way of thinking.

EMOTIONAL APPEAL

Words are effective when they evoke feelings. Emotional words and images are used to create a strong reaction in readers or viewers of ads and speeches.

> **Example:** A television scene of a large family gathered around the Thanksgiving dinner table. Uncles, aunts, cousins, and grandparents all talk and smile happily. They pause and clap as Mom places a huge baked turkey on the table. A voice-over says, "When the best of the season calls for the best in cooking, don't settle for anything but Best turkeys by Eiderdown Farms."

In nonfiction writing, an author will use powerful, descriptive words and images to affect a reader emotionally. This can be an appeal with positive emotions or with negative emotions.

> **Example:** The mother dolphin glided like a gray arrow alongside our boat. Leaning to one side, her bright round eye looked at us with a twinkle of pride, mischief and

© Copyright American Book Company. DO NOT DUPLICATE. 1-888-264-5877.

humor, all in one. She seemed to be sharing with us her delight in her baby, who glided next to her with the perfect harmony and grace of a Blue Angel. That magical experience on a dolphin cruise was the beginning of my commitment to preserving and protecting the oceans.

RHETORICAL QUESTION

Rhetorical questions do not expect an answer; they just set the listener up to think about the answer. And that answer usually reminds the listener of a need or a want. Advertising is based on needs and wants. Once the listener has thought of the need, the advertiser can respond with a solution to that need.

> **Example:** "Do you have blemishes that threaten to destroy your social life?" (Answer: "Well, I guess. Maybe. Sometimes...) "Then you need BeeTee, the Blemish Terminator made from bee pollen..."

In nonfiction, an author may use a **rhetorical question** to make the reader think about a situation or idea. If the question is asked in the right way, it prepares the reader to be willing to hear more about what the author has to say.

> **Example:** The growing number of power cars on our roads are choking our atmosphere and clogging our lungs. What can we do to save the air, breathe more freely, and still enjoy driving good cars? Your federal representative will be debating that and other questions of energy use this week in Congress. Your voice can be part of that debate if you write today to your congressional representative.

REPETITION

Have you ever had a song stuck in your head? If you listen to a song enough times, it can sometimes refuse to leave your memory, and you must hum it to yourself in spite of your best efforts. Advertisers rely on this phenomenon. They would love to have their slogans playing like a broken record in your mind. At the very least, they would like you to remember the elements of their messages. So, they use repetition.

> **Example:** "Call 806-900-0098 for your free in-home demonstration of the incredible product. That's 806-900-0098 for the product of a lifetime. Remember, that's 806-900-0098. Call now. 806-900-0098...!!

In nonfiction and in public speaking, authors and speakers often use repetition of an idea. This technique adds to the author's or speaker's effectiveness in persuading a reader or audience.

> **Example:** "As we graduate, we cannot just coast. We must go all-out to use the knowledge we've gained. We must go all-out to enter programs of higher learning that will take us to the next level. We must go all-out to find the work that will fulfill us and benefit our communities."

GLITTERING GENERALITIES

Glittering generalities are descriptions that sound great but are vague and unprovable praises of a product, an issue, or a person.

> **Example:** "Our candidate is a true American and has the strong family values this country needs." The label "true American" has no definition. It just sounds like a good thing to be. The same holds true for "family values." Values are different in different cultures and age groups, so who can define them?

Practice 2: Recognizing Argument Techniques

Read the following passages. After each passage, write which argument technique is being used in that passage. Then briefly explain your choice based on the description of these techniques presented in this chapter.

1. Do you want the state government to tax even more of your income? Don't let greedy Uncle Sam pocket more of your money. Write to your representative today, and send a "no more taxes" message to the leaders of our state.

_____

_____

2. The future of space exploration and safety rests with the continued orbit of the space stations. All people realize that life must continue to grow outward, to reach for the stars, and not be content to stay safely on the ground while the entire universe waits, unexplored. Threats to Earth's security continue to fill the outer regions of our stratosphere. There are exploding meteors, falling space junk, and even spot rays, to name only a few. Don't fall behind in the efforts to understand and protect ourselves from our universal environment. Space station programs need your support. Join the millions of citizens who care about Earth security. Be among the first to invest in the inevitable space travel opportunities that are just around the corner for all who are willing to support it. Send letters of support and donations to your congressional leadership today!

_____

_____

3. This is how we are exploiting animals on this earth. Millions of animals undergo cruel treatment in unsanitary research laboratories. They are caged, addicted to drugs, and sometimes killed and dissected in these laboratories. Animals that perform in circuses, television, movies, and even zoos often suffer neglect, boredom, and harsh abuse at the hands of their trainers. Fox, beaver, and mink caught in traps for their fur suffer a slow, painful death. Racing greyhounds are often killed once they can no longer compete, and only a few find homes through greyhound rescue organizations. - Excerpt from Animal Rights pamphlet

_____

_____

4. Many of the most famous names in the music industry are going public in their support of the newest CD technology. Storing capacity on the new CDs is greater than ever, and the clarity of sound will never be beat. Giants of the music industry are clamoring to be the first to take advantage of the new Super-CD technology. "I've never heard such trueness of timber," marvels conductor Victor von Caranova of the Kiev String Ensemble. "It rocks!" enthuses rock star Ashlee Thompson. Now the same technology used by the great recording studios of the world is available to you to use on your own home computer. Hear your favorite artists as you've never heard them before — and how they want to be heard!

_____

_____

5. What we need in the United States is not division; what we need in the United States is not hatred; what we need in the United States is not violence or lawlessness; but love and wisdom, and compassion toward one another, and a feeling of justice toward those who still suffer within our country, whether they be white or they be black. – Robert F. Kennedy

_____

_____

CHAPTER 5 SUMMARY

- An author's **viewpoint** is the author's perspective and feeling about a topic.

- An author's viewpoint may be **objective**, based on fact, or **biased**, based on opinion.

- The **evidence** the author presents plays an important role in convincing the reader about an author's viewpoint.

- **Argument techniques** are used in both **advertising** and **persuasive writing.**

- Learning to recognize various argument techniques helps you **understand** and **evaluate** what you are reading.

CHAPTER 5 REVIEW

1. **Cut 'n' Paste**. Collect a week's worth of newspaper articles, magazine ads, and editorials. See how many different types of argument techniques you can find and name. Cut out five ads and editorials, tape each to a piece of paper, and write what type(s) of argument techniques are used on the paper by the example. Under the type, briefly explain the author's viewpoint and any evidence the author uses to help persuade. Bring your examples to class and discuss you findings.

2. **Be the Persuasive Writer**. Write one example of an ad and one example of persuasive writing, using a different technique for each of them. Think about what your viewpoint will be. Then decide which technique you will use to fulfill the purpose. Write your passages at least seven sentences in length. Remember to include evidence to support your points. Bring your passages to class. The class will discuss how successful each persuasive technique is and may vote on the most convincing persuasive passage.

3. The following passage contains both an objective and a biased viewpoint. Read this passage, and identify the biased and objective sections. Then explain the reasons for your choices in a 7 – 8 sentence paragraph.

Animal Sacrifices

Every year, the U. S. military sends shoppers to Europe. These shoppers are looking for a very special product: well-bred, intelligent German shepherds or other dogs, suitable for use by U.S. armed forces. These government shoppers have a lot of money to spend: money that comes from the taxes each American citizen pays. They need a lot of money. They have to spend at least $3,000 for each dog. And they buy more than 300 dogs. These canine prizes are shipped back to the United States and trained in military camps for 100 days. After they graduate, they take on some of the most dangerous work any soldier can do. Often, they are in the line of fire, along with their trainers. Many dogs suffer terribly and die on duty. In Vietnam alone, hundreds of dogs were killed in battle. Most military dogs brought to Vietnam never returned. Here at home, you would not want your pet to be put in harm's way on purpose. We have animal protection laws to prevent that. However, these laws don't seem to apply to all dogs.

Chapter 6
Author's Purpose

This chapter covers Minnesota Reading Standard(s):

I.C.14	Students will critically read and evaluate to determine author's purpose, point of view, audience and message.

The MCA II Grade 8 Reading Test will require you to show that you can analyze texts, including different types of literature. What does it mean to analyze a text? It means to look carefully at *why* and *how* the text was written. What was the author's purpose in writing the text? How did the author present a viewpoint? Asking yourself these questions and the questions below will get you started in the process of analyzing literature.

- What is the author's **purpose**, or **motivation** for writing the text?
- Who is the **audience** the author has in mind?
- What is the author's **point of view** in the text?
- What is the author's **message** or **theme** in the text?

In this chapter, the **bolded** terms in the questions above will be defined and explained. You will see how authors use purpose, point of view, audience, and message to communicate ideas and information to their readers.

AUTHOR'S PURPOSE

Taking notes, sending e-mail, instant messaging, writing class essays: these are some of the many reasons why we write. Some reasons are fun, like writing in each other's yearbooks at the end of the school year. Other reasons, like writing out a shopping list, are not that much fun but must be done. Every time you write, you have a **purpose** or reason for writing. The same is true for all authors. An author's purpose for writing may be to **inform**, to **entertain**, to **motivate**, to **persuade**, and so on.

Author's Purpose

You can identify an **author's purpose** or motivation from the way the author writes. Here is an example of two different purposes in writing: Two students write articles about water for the school newsletter. One student writes about ways to conserve water at home. This author's purpose in writing the article is *to inform* readers about how to save water. The second student writes an opinion-based article about the importance of preserving water. This author's purpose for writing is *to persuade* readers to accept the author's point of view on water preservation.

Reporter - may write to inform, describe an event, or to relate an experience	 John Steinbeck	Literary author- may write to entertain, to create a mood, or to describe feelings

See if you can find out the author's purpose in writing the following two paragraphs.

1. The Labrador retriever is known to be a reliable, friendly, and loyal breed of dog. The male "Lab" grows to 22–24 inches in height, the female to 21–23 inches. The Lab has a waterproof coat of hair made up of two layers: a soft under layer and a top layer of "guard hairs." Labs can be black or chocolate in color, as well as golden. Since Labs are obedient and easily trained, they make good hunting dogs, watch dogs, and search and rescue dogs. Labs live to be about 10–12 years of age. They are low-maintenance pets. A lot of love and attention, exercise, and a good brush every week to prevent shedding will keep a Lab healthy and happy for many years.

2. Uncle Tate came by our house unexpectedly last Saturday morning. He was wearing a grin that stretched from ear to ear. He was also wearing his usual flight jacket and boots that clattered on the flagstone floor as he marched into the house past my dad. Uncle Tate stopped and, with a flourish, pulled a small golden puppy with bright chocolate eyes out from under the jacket. As he set it on the floor, the puppy began to bounce up and down and wiggle all over at the same time. Going to our knees to stroke the puppy and to get acquainted, we could hear the growls from our father and the replies from Uncle Tate passing overhead.

"If you think you are going to leave that animal here, you've been in too many tailspins."

"And if you don't think those kids need a dog, you haven't been in enough!"

Both paragraphs above discuss animals, but they do so in very different ways. Paragraph 1 provides basic information about an animal. The author's tone is fact-based with no emotion or dialog. The author's purpose in this paragraph is *to inform*.

In paragraph 2, on the other hand, the author writes in a descriptive tone. The author describes characters, actions, and events. The author uses expressive words and dialog. The author's purpose in paragraph 2 is *to entertain*.

If you can identify the author's purpose in writing a text, it will add greatly to your understanding of the text. Become familiar with the following list. It will help you better understand and describe the reason why an author writes.

Author's Purpose		
Purpose	**Definition**	**Sample Title**
To inform	To present facts	"Life Cycle of the Armadillo"
To entertain	To offer enjoyment	"My Baby-Sitting Disasters"
To persuade	To encourage action	"The Importance of Outdoor Play"
To instruct	To teach about a subject	"How to Groom Your Dog"
To create suspense	To convey uncertainty	"Spats, the Ferret, Disappears"
To motivate	To encourage to act	"Join the Environment Club!"
To cause doubt	To question the accepted	"Are Student Lunches Healthy?"
To describe an event	To narrate	"My First Day in High School"
To teach a lesson	To relate knowledge	"Mastering Verb Phrases"
To introduce a character	To describe a person's traits	"Sue Clue, Private Eye"
To create a mood	To set up an atmosphere	"Terror in the Abandoned House"
To relate an adventure	To tell an exciting story	"Lost on a Theme Park Field Trip"
To share a personal experience	To tell about an event in your life	"The Day My Sister Became My Friend"
To describe feelings	To show emotion through words	"My Brother Left for College Today"

Remember, you cannot always sum up the author's purpose in one word: "The author's purpose is to _____." Read a passage more than once. Look not only for the author's purpose but also for statements that describe that purpose. For instance, in the previous passage about dogs, you might identify and describe the authors' motives in the following ways:

Author's Purpose

Passage 1: The author's purpose is *to inform* readers *about the characteristics of a Labrador retriever.*

Passage 2: The author's purpose is *to entertain* readers *with a story about an unexpected gift.*

Practice 1: Author's Purpose

Read the passages below. Choose the best description of the author's purpose from the four possible descriptions given after each passage. Discuss your choices with your class or instructor.

Excerpt from Introduction to *Frankenstein*
by Mary Shelly

I busied myself to think of a story — a story to rival those which had excited us to this task. One which would speak to the mysterious fears of our nature and awaken thrilling horror—one to make the reader dread to look round, to curdle the blood, and quicken the beatings of the heart. If I did not accomplish these things, my ghost story would be unworthy of its name.

1. The author's purpose is to

   A. relate the story of a frightening event.

   B. describe what the author thinks would make a good horror story.

   C. teach a lesson in writing horror stories.

   D. persuade the reader that her story is a good one to read at night.

Excerpt from *Tom Sawyer*
by Mark Twain

Huckleberry was cordially hated and dreaded by all the mothers of the town, because he was idle and lawless and vulgar and bad and because all their children admired him so, and delighted in his forbidden society, and wished they dared to be like him. Tom was like the rest of the respectable boys, in that he envied Huckleberry his gaudy outcast condition, and was under strict orders not to play with him. So he played with him every time he got a chance.

2. The author's purpose is to

   A. teach a lesson about obeying parents.

   B. create a mood of intolerance in a small American town.

   C. introduce a character who is both loved and hated.

   D. describe an event in a child's life.

Remembering Sparks

It was 8 a.m. when I let Sparks, our young miniature pincher, into her "kingdom." Her enthusiastic barking had been waking the family. I thought I would let her entertain herself for a while so that the rest of the family could sleep in, bundled up, as they were, against the frosty New Year's Day morning outside. I left Sparks as her formal inspection of the garage began. In the garage, Sparks was in charge. For my part, I checked the cat door, knowing that it tended to come unhinged in cold weather. I thought it was locked. I was mistaken.

Sparks was nothing if not curious, and a loose cat door was all the invitation to adventure that she needed. Sadly, we searched for her in the frozen woods around our house for three days. We had named her Sparks because of her love of life, her excitement, and her constant curiosity. We lost her because of those same endearing characteristics.

3. The author's purpose is to

   A. share a personal experience about a sad day.

   B. entertain with an amusing story about a dog.

   C. instruct readers about a breed of dogs.

   D. motivate readers to adopt miniature pinchers.

Excerpt from "The Great Society" Speech
Lyndon Baines Johnson

A third place to build the Great Society is in the classrooms of America. There your children's lives will be shaped. Our society will not be great until every young mind is set free to scan the farthest reaches of thought and imagination….But more classrooms and more teachers are not enough. We must seek an educational system which grows in excellence as it grows in size. This means better training for our teachers.

4. The author's purpose is to

   A. instruct readers about the daily life of students.

   B. share a personal experience that took place in school.

   C. entertain readers with stories.

   D. persuade readers about what can make a nation great.

A Trip to Remember

My mother has crazy ideas sometimes. One year after having moved to St. Louis Park, Minnesota, she decided it was time to visit Seattle again. We couldn't get a plane ticket to Seattle for the weekend, but that didn't stop her. She just bought tickets to San Francisco instead. "We'll wing it from there," she said. "Winging it" meant landing in San Francisco, taking a cab, and waiting in the Amtrak station until 2 a.m. for a train. Then, for 12 hours, the sleek, silver train took us north. But from the time we had left home we were not able to get in touch with anyone! We didn't have cell phones in those days;

nobody did. The station had no phone, there was no time at the airport, and the train never stopped long enough to give us time to find a phone booth, call home, and dash back to the train before it departed. My dad didn't know where we were for a whole day. But I knew. I remember sleeping in the passenger car and buying soup in the restaurant car. I vividly recall watching the rising sun outside the window, the passing mountains, and glimpses of the ocean. And I especially remember the feeling of secret adventure, of being aware that no one knew where I was. It was the best trip I've ever had.

5. The author's purpose is to

    A. motivate readers to travel by plane.

    B. instruct readers on how to reach Seattle from St. Louis Park.

    C. relate an adventure from the author's childhood.

    D. avoid suspense about the fate of the travelers.

Practice 2: Author's Purpose – Using Supplemental Texts

In a group or on your own, find four fiction and four nonfiction selections from books, newspapers, or magazines. Use the list of authors' purposes from this section to identify the author's purpose in each selection. In some cases, the selection may have more than one purpose. Show evidence to support your responses. Exchange your passages with a classmate. Compare your responses and supporting evidence with your classmate. Then discuss your findings with the class or with your teacher.

AUDIENCE

Once authors are clear about their purpose for writing, they must consider their audience — the person(s) who will read what they write. No matter what the piece of writing will be, there is always an audience of some type. It can be one particular person, a specific group of people, or a larger unknown audience. Knowing the audience gives authors information that is important to consider when making decisions about the way they will write. For instance, if an author is writing about the planets, it is vitally important to know if the audience for the book is elementary school children or college astronomy majors. Some factors an author will consider include the following:

- the audience's **interest**: what topics or information is of interest to the audience,

- the audience's **prior knowledge**: what the audience already knows about the topic,

- the audience's **vocabulary**: language that the readers will understand,

- what the audience **needs and wants to know**: predicting the information or explanations that the audience wants.

In the case of persuasive writing such as editorials and opinion articles, the author needs to consider the position the audience is likely to be currently supporting. By considering the audience's current position, the author can anticipate objections and address those arguments in the article. Imagine if you were trying to persuade your friends to go to a new amusement park near your home. You would probably mention the great rides and entertainment it has to offer and tell them what a great time you are sure to have there. You might want to remind them that the price for everything, except for lunch, is included in the daily admission. However, if you were trying to persuade your parents to take your entire family, you might focus on the fact that it is very safe for your younger brothers and sisters and that your parents deserve to have a day of fun, too. For your parents, you might want to avoid mentioning how much it will cost!

Read the following two paragraphs written by the same person. Try to develop a picture of the audience that the writer had in mind.

> Since you're in the market for a new car, I wanted to tell you about mine. My new car is the best one I've owned. It's a 2006 Puma. It's got a 5.0 overhead cam engine with multi-port fuel injection. It can do 0 – 60 mph in 5 seconds. With that much engine, passing cars on the highway is a breeze, but handling corners on back roads is a little trickier than with my old truck. I love the rush I get when I'm cruising around with my new wheels. You should consider buying one, too.

> Since you're in the market for a new car, I wanted to tell you about mine. My new car is the best one I've owned. It's a 2006 Puma. This sporty two-door is canary yellow with electric blue racing stripes and silver mag wheels. It has cordovan leather seats and a concert hall-quality sound system. The sunroof is the perfect finishing touch. You should see the looks I get when I'm cruising around with my new wheels. You should consider buying one, too.

In both paragraphs, the author is telling someone about a new car, but each paragraph includes very different details about the car. Based on these differences, how would you describe the intended audience of each paragraph? What evidence is there for your description?

AUDIENCE INTEREST

How does the writer try to catch the audience's interest in each paragraph? Clearly, the first paragraph is intended for a reader who is interested in a car's power and performance. So, the writer describes the car's engine, as well as the car's speed and handling. The second paragraph, on the other hand, mentions nothing about performance. The writer assumes that the audience is concerned with appearance and style, so the description focuses on colors and high-priced options.

AUDIENCE KNOWLEDGE

What does the writer assume that the audience already knows? Since the reader of the first paragraph is interested in performance, the writer assumes that the reader knows what a Puma is and that going 0 – 60 mph in 5 seconds is fast. The reader of the second paragraph may need the author to describe the Puma as a "sporty two-door," but the reader understands well the stunning colors and fine accessories of the new car.

AUDIENCE VOCABULARY

What kinds of words will the audience be familiar with and understand easily? The writer expects the reader of the first paragraph to know technical terms like "5.0 L" and "multi-port fuel injection." While these terms may speak loudly and clearly to the reader of the first paragraph, they may mean nothing to the reader of the second paragraph who appreciates "cordovan leather" and a "concert-hall-quality sound system." Likewise, the reader of the first paragraph may have no use for these terms since they have nothing to do with power or performance.

WHAT THE AUDIENCE SHOULD KNOW

What does the writer want the audience to know? In both paragraphs, the writer wants to share excitement about a new car purchase in order to encourage readers to purchase the same kind of car. The writer shares information that will be of interest to two kinds of audiences and that will encourage readers to purchase a Puma. As a reader you need to be aware of the writer's intentions; what does the writer seem to think you know? In some cases as you are reading, you should ask yourself "what does the author NOT want me to know?" In some cases, an author may purposely withhold certain information from the audience.

When an author is considering how to convey what he or she thinks the audience needs to know, the author must take into consideration the audience's interests, prior knowledge, and vocabulary skill.

Various writing assignments or "real-life" writing situations will require you to address a particular audience, such as parents, teachers, other students, or the editor of a local newspaper. Considering your audience will help you write more effectively too.

Practice 3: Audience

For each of the following topics, describe the interest, knowledge, and vocabulary of the given audience, as well as what you think the audience should know, and its possible current position. An example to guide you follows.

Sample Topic: Parental Advisory Stickers on Music CDs

Audience: **parents**
Audience Interest: **interested in the welfare of their children**
Audience Knowledge: **unfamiliar with specific artists, but aware of rude music**
Audience Vocabulary: **some knowledge of teen vocabulary, but mostly not**
Audience Should Know: **parents, not record companies, need to take responsibility**
Possible Current Position: **in favor of all music having detailed warnings**

1. Topic: Parental Advisory Stickers on music CDs   Audience: students

2. Topic: High Salaries of Professional Athletes   Audience: baseball player

3. Topic: High Salaries of Professional Athletes   Audience: stadium worker

4. Topic: Importance of a High School Diploma   Audience: high school dropout

5. Topic: Importance of a High School Diploma   Audience: employer

POINT OF VIEW

A story's **point of view** is the perspective or outlook from which a story is told. There may be a character narrating the story, or there may be an unidentified speaker describing the action and thoughts of all main characters. For example, Mary Shelley writes *Frankenstein* from the first person point of view, but she uses three different narrators to tell their own stories: Dr. Frankenstein, the creator of the monster; the monster himself; and Walton, the last man to speak to both.

THREE TYPES OF POINT OF VIEW

First Person
In the **first person**, a narrator tells the story from the "I" point of view. In *The House On Mango Street*, Esperanza tells her story as the main character. Likewise, in *Shiloh*, Marty Preston, the main character, narrates the story about himself and a dog.

Second Person
In the **second person**, the speaker is talking to you and uses the pronoun "you." This is not often used on its own, but the second person reference is fairly common in poetry, short essays, and songs. For example, the songs "You Are My Sunshine" and "You've Got a Friend."

Third Person
The speaker tells a story describing characters as "he," "she," or "they" as in *The Pearl* by John Steinbeck.

- **omniscient**
Omniscient means "all-knowing." In the **third person omniscient**, the narrator is capable of knowing, telling, and seeing all that happens to the main characters. In Guy de Maupassant's "The Necklace," the third person speaker describes all the story action and the inner thoughts of the main characters.

- **limited**
In the **third person limited** point of view, the speaker tells the story knowing only what is seen, heard, and felt by the thoughts and viewpoint of one character, usually the main character. In Crane's *Red Badge of Courage*, the author tells the story through the soldier, Henry. We experience the events through Henry's eyes and ears.

Deciding what point of view the author is using to tell a story is a first big step in understanding how that story will work. When you determine what the point of view is, you are ahead in understanding how the frame for the story will be set.

The choice of narrator affects the **credibility of a text**. The credibility of a text simply means how believable the story is for the reader. Is the voice true to the character, the place of the story, and the time of the story? If the answer to these questions is yes, then the voice helps the story become believable to the reader. One example of a credible text is Phyllis Reynold's *Shiloh*. Naylor's narrator is a boy whose voice reflects the time and place of the story.

A first person narrator who is very honest and clear-sighted, such as Naylor's Marty, may be well trusted in telling a story. This point of view, however, is limited to the narrator's experience and feelings only. The same holds true for the limited third person. For example, in Stephen Crane's *The Red Badge of Courage*, only one character, the young soldier, is understood completely. The third person omniscient is the most knowing position for a narrator. However, does this narrator simply give the facts and details to the reader and let the reader make decisions about the story, or does the narrator state an opinion and expect the reader to agree? A believable narrator will let readers decide what they think about a story. An example of this type of narration is John Steinbeck's novel *Of Mice and Men*.

Practice 4: Point of View

Skim through your literature book, a collection of short stories. Find two examples of first person, third person omniscient, and third person limited points of view. Read a few paragraphs of each, listening to the "feel" of the narration. Which point of view do you like the most? Explain why. Record your thoughts on paper. Then share them with your teacher or classmates.

THEME

Whereas facts and specific examples usually support the main idea of a nonfiction passage, more subtle details like images, characters, and events reveal the main idea of a fictional passage. We use the word **message** or **theme** in discussing the main idea of short stories, novels, poetry and plays. Look at the example below:

Excerpt from *The Red Badge of Courage*
by Stephen Crane

The youth gave a shriek as he confronted the thing. He was, for moments, turned to stone before it. He remained staring into the liquid-looking eyes. The dead man and the living man exchanged a long look. Then the youth cautiously put one hand behind him and brought it against a tree. Leaning upon this he retreated, step by step, with his face still toward the thing. He feared that if he turned his back the body might spring up and stealthily pursue him.

Which of the following statements is the message or theme for the passage?

A. The living and the dead form bonds of love.

B. Death should not be feared.

C. Never speak badly about the dead.

D. Confronting death can be terrifying.

While the first three choices contain general truths, they do not apply specifically to this passage. For example, *A* focuses on love between the living and the dead, while the details in the passage convey fear and dread. Likewise, *B* ignores the fear so apparent in the description. Finally, *C* is incorrect because the youth never speaks badly about the dead person. His shock is so great that all he can do is shriek in fear.

Therefore, answer *D* is the best choice. It describes the overall message of the passage and is based upon the details presented

---

Tips for Finding the Theme
1. **Read** the passage carefully.
2. **Think** of one statement that summarizes the overall message of what you read.
3. **Write** your answer, or compare your answer with the choices given.
4. **Make sure the details in the passage support your answer.** Sometimes a statement may be true but not relevant to the passage.
5. **Make sure your answer summarizes** the message of the entire passage, not just one part.

Practice 5: Theme

Read the following passages. Then choose the best statement of the theme.

1.   As the old man walked the beach at dawn, he noticed a young man ahead of him picking up starfish and flinging them into the sea. Finally, catching up with the youth, he asked why he was doing this. The young man explained that the stranded starfish would die if left until the morning sun.

      "But the beach goes on for miles, and there are millions of starfish," commented the old man. "How can your effort make any difference?"

      The young man looked at the starfish in his hand and then threw it safely in the waves. "It makes a difference to this one," he said.

– Anonymous

A.   The morning sun will kill stranded starfish.

B.   Starfish must be saved from extinction.

C.   Saving even one life can make a difference.

D.   Saving millions of starfish is a waste of time.

2.   In *Between Parent and Teenager*, Dr. Haim Ginott told this story: As Jean walked along the beach with her mother, she asked, "Mom, how do you hold a husband after you've found him?"

      Her mother gave her a silent lesson in love. She scooped up two handfuls of sand. One she squeezed hard. The more she squeezed, the more sand escaped. The other she held lightly, and the sand remained.

Jean said, "I see."

A. Learn the dangers of love.

B. Learn the principles of sand science.

C. Learn the many themes of love.

D. Learn the difference between love and possessiveness.

3.

An old male elephant was dying in the African wilderness. A group of elephants from his herd gathered around this male, trying to get him to stand up. They tried to stroke him with their trunks, raise him with their tusks, and put food in his mouth. Nothing seemed to work, so the herd left. However, a mother and her calf remained, standing with their backs to the dead elephant. The mother tried to touch the dead elephant with one foot. Then the herd returned and began circling the dead companion. After a time, they gathered tree branches and grass clumps scattering these items on or around the body.

A. Elephants often die alone in the wilderness.

B. Some animals perform rituals to mourn their dead.

C. Death is a fact of life in the African wilderness.

D. The elephant population in Africa is declining because they are hunted and killed.

4.

A man was going down from Jerusalem to Jericho, when he fell into the hands of robbers. They stripped him of his clothes, beat him, and went away, leaving him half dead. A priest happened to be going down the same road, and when he saw the man, passed by on the other side. So too, a Levite, when he came to the place and saw him, passed by on the other side. But a Samaritan, as he traveled, came where the man was; and when he saw him, he took pity on him. He went to him and bandaged his wounds, pouring on oil and wine. Then he put the man on his own donkey, took him to an inn and took care of him. The next day he took out two silver coins and gave them to the innkeeper. "Look after him," he said, "and when I return, I will reimburse you for any extra expense you may have."

– *The Bible*

A. Robbers can be dangerous on the roads.

B. Try to avoid areas where there is crime.

C. Innkeepers take good care of their customers.

D. A good neighbor loves those in need.

5.   Allie was quite bright, and after a few years, her
job was just that, a job. Allie wanted a career. So she
went back to school at night while she worked.
After graduating, she got a position with a company
as a computer programmer. It was challenging, and
Allie was good at it. Allie was promoted within two
years and transferred to the corporate headquarters
in Minnesota. Moving to another state was difficult.
Allie didn't know anyone, and she was young, 28
years old. All the people in her work group were
men in their 40s who were already married. Allie

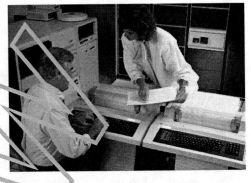

decided to pour herself into her work for a while and try to get promoted and transferred
again. Allie worked hard, and it paid off. They offered her a promotion and a transfer to Fort
Worth, Texas. There was only one problem. She was in love.

A.   Working hard brings happiness.

B.   Education results in better job opportunities.

C.   Choosing between a career and a relationship is a challenge.

D.   In today's society, promotions occur more often than in the past.

Practice 6. Identifying Message or Theme

Read the following passages. Then write a statement for each passage that summarizes the theme. Compare
your responses with your group, class, or instructor.

Excerpt from *Life in the Iron Mills*
by Rebecca Davis

1.   It was market day. The narrow window of the jail looked
down directly on the carts and wagons drawn up in a long
line, where they had unloaded. He could see, too, and hear
distinctly the clink of money as it changed hands, the busy
crowd of whites and blacks shoving, pushing one another, and
the haggling and swearing at the stalls. Somehow, the sound
more than anything else had done, wakened him up,—made
the whole world real to him. He was done with the world and
the business of it. He let the tin fall, and looked out, pressing
his face close to the rusty bars. How they crowded and
pushed! And he,—he should never walk that pavement again!

_____

_____

Author's Purpose

2.

All the World's a Stage

Stella and her new friend, Max, were in line for lunch in the cafeteria. Everyone was eating their food without making too much noise. Max had just finished telling Stella about the self-defense class he was taking after school. Stella asked Max, "Why don't you show me one of the special self-defense moves you learned?"

"Sure," Max said. "Just watch this." Max, full of concentration, tilted his head forward and slammed it into his cafeteria tray. Stella and the rest of the lunch room looked up in shock to see that Max had broken the cafeteria tray, and the skin on his forehead was wide open.

"Are you OK?" Stella asked as Max recovered from his display of power.

"Of course I am," Max said as he lost balance and crashed to the floor.

"What does breaking a cafeteria tray have to do with self-defense?" Stella asked. Max could not respond. He could only see stars spinning quickly around his head.

When Max returned from the hospital, he was just fine except for the thin line of stitches he had on his forehead. One day, several weeks later, Max was once again in line next to Stella at lunch. He turned to her and said, "That self-defense move turned out badly. Let me show you a new move I learned in gymnastics class!"

"Please," Stella said. "No more special tricks. Just be yourself, and stick to what you do best."

3.

The Little Girl Who Knew CPR

Little Zack went outside and walked around the swimming pool. There was something shiny on the bottom, and when he looked closer, he fell in the water. His sister, Penny, was making her little brother a peanut butter and jelly sandwich when she heard the splash. Seeing that her brother was nowhere in sight, Penny ran outside.

When Penny arrived at the pool, she saw that her brother was motionless at the bottom. Quickly, Penny jumped in and brought Zack to the surface. At nine years old, Penny had just taken a CPR course at her school in her gym class. She immediately started doing what she had learned. Zack was not breathing and did not have a pulse. She turned Zack's head upwards and began doing chest compressions and mouth-to-mouth resuscitation. At this moment, Penny's mom came outside looking for her children. "Mom, call 911. Zack fell into the pool," Penny yelled. Penny's mom ran back inside and did what she was told. Penny's CPR had worked. Zack spit out the water quickly. Soon, Zack's pulse returned, and he was breathing on his own.

By the time the ambulance arrived, Zack's color had returned to his face, and he could talk. The paramedics were amazed that this little girl had saved her brother's life. Instantly, the girl became a celebrity at school, and the school threw a party for her and the firemen who had taught her class CPR.

_____

_____

4.

Mowing the Grass — a Tragedy

One sunny day, Allen went outside to mow the lawn for his parents. Quickly, he started the motor and began mowing. "I bet I can finish this whole lawn in under thirty minutes!" Allen said. Because he was mowing so quickly, Allen did not notice the large rock in the middle of the lawn. He did not think to clear the lawn of sticks and rocks before he started mowing. The rock entered his lawn mower with a *crunch* and broke apart the blade. Rock fragments pelted Allen in his shoes and ankles. Allen cried out aloud, saying, "Ouch. My ankle really hurts. My new shoes are all messed up. Now I can't even mow the grass. I'll never mow the lawn so quickly again."

_____

_____

Practice 7: Writing Theme or Message Statements

On your own or in a group, review any four stories from your literature book. Write a message or theme statement for each one. In some cases, you may find more than one message or theme in a story. Then compare your answers with the class or instructor.

CHAPTER 6 SUMMARY

- An author's **purpose** is the reason for writing the text.

- An author's purpose may be to **inform**, to **entertain**, or to **persuade**. Other purposes are also possible.

- An author must also consider the **audience** to be reached.

- A skilled author will consider the **interest**, **prior knowledge**, **vocabulary**, and **needs** of the audience.

- Knowing an author's **point of view** or **outlook** is important for understanding a story or article.

- An author's **message** or **theme** is the main idea or point the author wants to communicate to the audience.

- In some cases, an author can convey several different messages in the same piece of writing.

CHAPTER 6 REVIEW

Directions: For each of the following readings, circle the correct purpose, audience, point of view, and message.

1.
Excerpt from The Words of Chief Joseph
by Chief Joseph

Whenever the white man treats the Indian as they treat each other, then we will have no more wars. We shall all be alike—brothers of one father and one mother, with one sky above us and one country around us, and one government for all. Then the Great Spirit Chief who rules above will smile upon this land, and send rain to wash out the bloody spots made by brothers' hands from the face of the earth. For this time the Indian race is waiting and praying. I hope that no more groans of wounded men and women will ever go to the ear of the Great Spirit Chief above, and that all people may be one people.

Purpose:

A. to entertain   B. to describe   C. to inspire

Audience:

A. Native Americans   B. Americans   C. white Americans

Point of View:

A. first person   B. second person   C. third person

Message:

A. Mutual respect and fairness will unite people together.

B. The Great Spirit Chief rules over heaven and earth.

C. Unity comes from the Great Spirit.

D. The White Man's government belongs to the Indian race.

2.
Spotlight on Olive Oil

Olive oil is an amazing liquid that has influenced the cultures of the Mediterranean for over 4,000 years. You can eat it, cook with it, and use it as a lubricant for squeaky doors. You can prepare fish, vegetables, herbs, and cheese with it. It is full of vitamin E and contains no cholesterol.

In the past, olive oil remained an exotic novelty that Italian, Greek, and Spanish immigrants used in their specialty dishes. In restaurants, most people thought olive oil used in cooking added a heavy, greasy flavor to food. At that time, olive oil was of poor quality and was often mixed with animal fat or other inferior oils.

In the 1970s, several new studies revealed that heart disease was uncommon among Mediterranean people who used olive oil. Researchers have found that olive oil is full of antioxidants which deter fatty deposits from forming in the arteries. In addition, olive oil is rich in mono-saturated fat—a good fat for your body.

Purpose:

   A.   to amuse   B.   to inform   C.   to criticize

Audience:

   A.   women   B.   children   C.   adults

Point of View:

   A.   first person   B.   second person   C.   third person

Message:

   A.   Drink olive oil every day.

   B.   Olive oil makes food taste better.

   C.   Using olive oil with food is a healthy and ancient practice.

3.

Moon Bound!

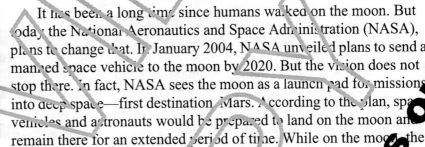

     It has been a long time since humans walked on the moon. But today the National Aeronautics and Space Administration (NASA), plans to change that. In January 2004, NASA unveiled plans to send a manned space vehicle to the moon by 2020. But the vision does not stop there. In fact, NASA sees the moon as a launch pad for missions into deep space—first destination Mars. According to the plan, space vehicles and astronauts would be prepared to land on the moon and remain there for an extended period of time. While on the moon, the space team would assemble a new space vehicle, which would make the journey to Mars.

     Launching the new vehicle from the moon would be easier than it would be from Earth. On Earth, it takes a lot of fuel to fire the thrusters to lift space vehicles off the ground and away from the pull of gravity. On the moon, there is far less gravity, and therefore, far less fuel would be needed. In fact, NASA scientists say that materials found right on the moon's soil could be a good source for rocket fuel. That source for fuel is important because the trip to Mars would be a long one. It could take up to three years to go there and back. Humans have never spent that much time in space.

     Scientists say that the crew of the spaceship would have to be larger than they have been in the past. That is because it is possible that in three years, crew members could become ill or even die. All possibilities have to be considered when planning a mission as ambitious as going to Mars. But NASA planners believe that it can be done by 2030. It looks as if aeronautics and space engineering might be a promising career over the next few decades.

Purpose:

   A.   to inform   B.   to create suspense   C.   to describe feelings

Audience:

   A.   astronauts   B.   scientists   C.   students

Point of View:

   A.   first person   B.   second person   C.   third person

Message:

   A.   Humans may one day live on the moon.

   B.   Soon astronauts will travel to the moon and Mars for a long period of time.

   C.   NASA scientists will build a space station on the moon.

4.

Would You Like Fries With That?

One of the reasons for obesity in America is the availability of what scientists call "energy dense foods." If food is "energy dense," it means that you get a lot of energy—calories—from a small amount of it. Scientists say that human beings were not designed to need much of this kind of food. When societies first started living by farming, they ate food that had a moderate fat content: vegetables, grains, fruits, and animals grown on the farm. Their bodies learned to use the energy from this kind of food to do their work. Now the dessert you have at lunch might contain more calories than what our ancestors ate in a whole meal. Scientists say that our bodies have not learned how to use that energy efficiently. So, our bodies convert the extra energy into fat. So ask your parents to stay away from the "energy-dense" food and to buy foods that your body can use! Reach for fruits and vegetables and refuse the fries.

Purpose:

   A.   to tell a story   B.   to inform   C.   to persuade

Audience:

   A.   parents   B.   teens   C.   senior citizens

Point of View:

   A.   first person   B.   second person   C.   third person

Message:

   A.   Eat healthy and avoid fat.

   B.   Farmers eat better and live longer.

   C.   Energy dense foods are popular everywhere.

5.

Excerpt from *The Dead*
by James Joyce

Yes, the newspapers were right: snow was general all over Ireland. It was falling on every part of the dark central plain, on the treeless hills, falling softly upon the Bog of Allen and, farther westward, softly falling into the dark mutinous Shannon waves. It was falling, too, upon every part of the lonely churchyard on the hill where Michael Furey lay buried. It lay thickly drifted on the crooked crosses and headstones, on the spears of the little gate, on the barren thorns. His soul swooned slowly as he heard the snow falling faintly through the universe and faintly falling, like the descent of their last end, upon all the living and the dead.

Purpose:

    A. to frighten   B. to create a mood   C. to teach a lesson

Audience:

    A. humanity   B. writers   C. children

Point of View:

    A. first person   B. second person   C. third person

Message:

    A. Snow in Ireland is unusual.

    B. Snow covers everything in a blanket of white.

    C. Dead people miss seeing snow in winter.

6.

Mr. Sanchez Makes His Rounds

It was midnight. Mr. Sanchez always made a final round of the barn at night to check that all was in order. He was later than usual tonight, and he shuffled more than walked, struggling to keep his eyes open. It was hard enough to see through the moonless gloom. For a moment, it seemed all was well. Horses stood in their stalls in quiet, unfathomable submission to the winter cold, dreaming, perhaps, of grassy fields. Then, "Aw, not brought in, tonight?" Mr. Sanchez thought, as he glimpsed two small equine shadows standing patiently at the pasture gate next to the barn's outer row of stalls. "Not doing their job," he mumbled, picking up one of the lead ropes always, it seemed, within reach. He made his way through the side passage out of the barn and towards the gate. He only needed one rope for the ponies. He knew that little Fantasia would stick like hoofed devotion to Midnight's side on the way back to their shared stall.

Mr. Sanchez opened the gate a little. "C'mon, big girl, let's go home," he coaxed. His gentle words had hardly passed his lips when they blended in the night air with unearthly screeches, snarls, and growls. A black, shapeless streak hurtled towards the small group from nowhere and everywhere at once as horrible screams and grunts wrenched themselves from some unnameable throat. In an instant, the world was full of black mane, hooves, tails, legs, screams, and terror. Mr. Sanchez had no sense of his body which had turned to jelly and had lost all connection with the earth beneath it. He was falling.

A stall! The thought pierced the fog of his panic. Ten paces away. He had no memory of covering the distance. Somehow he half dove, half flew over the stall door, and there he was, on his back, on a floor of wood shavings and dirt, eye-level with a set of palomino hooves. At his entrance, Sunshine, having almost panicked during the preceding moments of chaos outside her stall, had started nervously, and then calmed down. She snorted, regarding her owner from this new perspective with some interest. Mr. Sanchez looked back at her. She seemed to be wondering if, after all the upsetting commotion of moments ago, this clumsily delivered package at her feet was supposed to be her comic relief. After a minute, though, all interest waned, and she lipped up a clump of alfalfa from under her hanging grain bucket. Her ears relaxed back into their contented position, and life went on.

Mr. Sanchez pulled himself up against the stall door. A pig, he thought; it must have been a wild pig. Where in tarnation had that monster come from? For that matter, where in tarnation have the ponies disappeared to? He had work to do, he could see, but that could wait. When the coast was clear—*very* clear—he would call the sheriff and report the menace. But for now, he patted Sunshine. Her warm strength and simple contentment gave him confidence. Still rattled from his fright, he was in no hurry to leave.

Purpose:

   A.   to motivate   B.   to narrate   C.   to inform

Audience:

   A.   ranchers   B.   young people   C.   veterinarians

Point of View:

   A.   first person   B.   third person limited   C.   third person omniscient

Message:

   A.   Wild pigs often enter barns at night.

   B.   Caring for horses is very rewarding.

   C.   A barn is not always a place of peace and tranquility.

Chapter 7
Characters in Literature

This chapter covers Minnesota Reading Standard(s):

II.D.3	Students will analyze a character's traits, emotions, or motivations and give supporting evidence from the text.

LITERARY CHARACTERS

In a bicycle, the wheels, gears, and chain all work together to make the bike go. None of these parts would operate the same without the others. In fictional literary works, **characters**, the imaginary people, animals, or creatures that take part in the action of a work, tell each other and the reader about their ideas and feelings.

When the parts of a bicycle work together, they make the bicycle perform well. Similarly, the interaction or relationship between characters create a well written story. Through a character's words and actions, the story comes alive for readers.

There are different types of characters in a story. The **main characters** are the focus of a story; the story centers on their thoughts and actions. They are the most important characters. The **minor characters** may be friends, relatives, neighbors, and so on of the main character. They interact with the main characters and with one another, moving the action along and providing background for the story.

CHARACTER TYPES

Just as the parts of a bike have separate functions, so do different types of characters play different roles in a literary work. On the next page is a partial list of important character types.

Narrator   the person telling the story. The narrator will often be a main character. In *Roll of Thunder, Hear My Cry*, the narrator is Cassie Logan, and she is the main character. Sometimes another character or an outside voice narrates the story.

Protagonist   the main character(s). The protagonist is the character who leads the action, is involved in the conflict, and often changes by the end of the story. The protagonist is often the hero but not always. Many short stories by Edgar Allan Poe have protagonists who do evil things. A story can also have more than one protagonist. In "The Gift of the Magi," by O. Henry, both Della and Jim are the protagonists.

Antagonist   the character(s) working against the protagonist. The antagonist can also be a force battling the protagonist, such as nature or society. In Gary Paulsen's *The Hatchet*, the main character, Brian, struggles against nature to survive; nature is the antagonist. The antagonist is often the villain in the story but not always.

You are the main character, the protagonist, in your life story. There are minor characters in your life story as well. These people learn about you by what you say, what you do, and how you look. We learn about characters in fictional writing in the same ways.

CHARACTERIZATION

Characterization is the way we learn about characters in a story. A writer can reveal characters in five indirect ways (description, dialogue, actions, thoughts, observations), or in one very direct way (narration).

Description   An author describes how characters look and dress. The description of a character's appearance can reveal many things about the character. For example, this description of Scrooge from *A Christmas Carol* by Charles Dickens shows us the character's cold heart: "The cold within him froze his old features, nipped his pointed nose, shriveled his cheek, stiffened his gait; made his eyes red, his thin lips blue; and spoke out shrewdly in his grating voice."

Dialogue   An author lets us hear the characters speak. The conversations between characters (dialogue) allow us to learn more about the characters. When we read dialogue, we get to hear what the characters say as well as see how they respond to each other. When Scrooge says, "If I could work my will, every idiot who goes about with 'Merry Christmas' on his lips, should be boiled with his own pudding, and buried with a stake of holly through his heart," we learn how he feels about Christmas. The way in which characters speak can also tell us about them, especially when the author uses regional dialects, such as in this quote that demonstrates Scrooge's changed nature: "Sit ye down before the fire, my dear, and have a warm, Lord bless ye."

Actions   An author shows us what characters do. How characters act reveals a lot about their personalities. This quote from *A Christmas Carol* shows Scrooge acting in a very different manner than at the beginning of the story. "He went to church, and walked about the streets, and watched the people hurrying to and fro, and patted children on the head, and questioned beggars, and looked down into the kitchens of houses, and up to the windows, and found that everything could yield him pleasure."

Thoughts   An author lets us listen to characters' thoughts and feelings, which allow us to see their motivations, conflicts, and changes. For example, this quote from *A Christmas Carol* shows one character's transformation at the end of the story: "Scrooge hung his head to hear his own words quoted by the Spirit, and was overcome with penitence and grief. Its mysterious presence filled him with a solemn dread."

Observations   An author shows what other characters in the story say or think about a character. Scrooge's uncle says this of him: "He's a comical old fellow, that's the truth. And not so pleasant as he might be."

Narration   An author has the narrator tell us directly what a character is like. Dickens writes, "But he was a tight-fisted hand at the grindstone, Scrooge! a squeezing, wrenching, grasping, scraping, clutching, covetous, old sinner!"

Think for a moment about how you act with people you know and why you act that way. This will help you understand why a character acts a certain way.

CHARACTER INTERACTION

Getting to know characters is like getting to know new friends. We are interested in learning all about them, so we ask questions. We find out about fictional characters by asking ourselves questions about them during or after reading a selection.

Relationships   What kind of lives do the characters have? What have they experienced? The relationships characters have with family, work, and society show us more about them.

Motivations   Why do characters do what they do? What are the motivations or reasons that characters have for acting in a certain way? What characters want often motivates them to action. For example, a lonely character will want to gain friendship; an uncertain character will want to make a decision. Many things, such as fear, greed, love, or jealousy, can motivate characters.

Conflicts

What problems do the characters have? Stories have conflicts or problems that the characters must work out. How characters handle a problem says a lot about them. Do the characters run away from conflict? Do they try to work through problems? Some characters have internal conflicts: confusion inside themselves, decisions to make. Some characters have external conflicts to work out: problems with another character, struggles against nature, or problems with society.

Influences

What influences can change the characters? To make a story as real as possible, an author will describe influences that affect the story's characters. An influence is some outside pressure or force that can change the thoughts and actions of a character. How characters react to influences says a lot about the characters. If a character knows that a certain way of speaking could bring him success, this is an outside pressure that may change how the character speaks.

Across Five Aprils by Irene Hunt creates a fictional life for a fictional family, the Creightons, during the Civil War. Jethro and his sister Jenny are running their family's farm in southern Illinois, after their brothers have gone off to fight the war and their father has had a heart attack.

- **Relationships:** Jethro is a young boy forced by outside circumstances to become a man. Jenny is his older sister and his only companion during the war. Together they work to support their family and each other during the war. They understand each other's fears and worries.

- **Motivations:** Jethro wants to please his parents and teachers. He wants to prove that he is strong enough, both physically and emotionally, to run the family's farm.

- **Conflicts:** Jethro has an **internal conflict** (a conflict inside his mind) about the war. He is not sure how he feels about it and its effects on his family and the country. The Creighton family also has external conflicts with the townspeople who harass them when one of their sons goes to fight with the South.

- **Influences:** Jethro is greatly influenced by his teachers, Shadrach and Milton. They both guide Jethro and urge him to continue his education. Milton discusses the war with Jethro when he has trouble understanding or accepting it. Jethro is also influenced by President Lincoln and writes him a letter asking advice.

Chapter 7

Practice 1: Characters and Characterization

Read the following passage. Answer the questions that follow.

Excerpt from "The Bohemian Girl" by Willa Cather

The transcontinental express swung along the windings of the Sand River Valley, and in the rear seat of the observation car a young man sat greatly at his ease, not in the least discomfited by the fierce sunlight which beat in upon his brown face and neck and strong back. There was a look of relaxation and of great passivity about his broad shoulders, which seemed almost too heavy until he stood up and squared them. He wore a pale flannel shirt and a blue silk necktie with loose ends. His trousers

were wide and belted at the waist, and his short sack coat hung open. His heavy shoes had seen good service. His reddish-brown hair, like his clothes, had a foreign cut. He had deep-set, dark blue eyes under heavy reddish eyebrows. His face was kept clean only by close shaving, and even the sharpest razor left a glint of yellow in the smooth brown of his skin. His teeth and the palms of his hands were very white. His head, which looked hard and stubborn, lay indolently in the green cushion of the wicker chair, and as he looked out at the ripe summer country a teasing, not unkindly smile played over his lips. Once, as he basked thus comfortably, a quick light flashed in his eyes, curiously dilating the pupils, and his mouth became a hard, straight line, gradually relaxing into its former smile of rather kindly mockery. He told himself, apparently, that there was no point in getting excited; and he seemed a master hand at taking his ease when he could. Neither the sharp whistle of the locomotive nor the brakeman's call disturbed him. It was not until after the train had stopped that he rose, put on a Panama hat, took from the rack a small valise and a flute case, and stepped deliberately to the station platform. The baggage was already unloaded, and the stranger presented a check for a battered sole-leather steamer trunk.

1. Based on this passage, which of the following sentences best describes the man?
   A. The man is poorly dressed and feeling uncomfortable.
   B. The man is hard working and curious.
   C. The man is dressed strangely and very excited.
   D. The man is strong, relaxed, and a stranger in this place.

2. What does the following sentence say about the character? "His head, which looked hard and stubborn, lay indolently in the green cushion of the wicker chair, and as he looked out at the ripe summer country a teasing, not unkindly smile played over his lips."
   A. The character is tired from his long trip and wishes it were over.
   B. The character is a stubborn man and is feeling pleased.
   C. The character enjoys teasing people.
   D. The character's head is very large and strange looking.

3. What three methods of characterization are used to describe the man?

    A.   observation, dialogue, and narration

    B.   dialogue, description, and action

    C.   description, thought, and action

    D.   thought, observation, and narration

Practice 1:   Characters and Characterization

Choose a fictional work from your literature textbook. After reading your selection, complete the following activities on your own paper.

1. Describe the character types from the fictional work you selected. Who is the narrator? Who is the protagonist? Who or what is the antagonist?

2. Choose one main character from your fictional work, and describe how the author has shown the character. Which of the six methods of characterization did the author use to reveal the character? Then, describe the character completely by listing as many character traits as you can.

CHAPTER 7 SUMMARY

- **Characters** are the imaginary people, animals, or creatures that take part in the action of the story.

- Three important types of characters are the **narrator**, **protagonist**, and **antagonist**.

- Authors reveal characters by **description**, **dialogue**, **actions**, **thoughts**, **observations**, and **narration**.

- Characters interact with each other through **relationships**, **motivations**, **conflicts**, and **influences**.

CHAPTER 7 REVIEW

Read each of the passages, and answer the questions that follow.

"Dread" Locks

Elizabeth sat on the stool in the center of the room, terrified of moving. The scissors seemed to be on all sides of her.

She must be patient, she kept telling herself. No moving. Be good. One small move and she might lose an ear, or an eye. How much longer was this going to take? She realized she had been holding her breath and let a sigh escape.

"Be still," the voice said.

"Are you almost done?" she dared to ask.

"Yes, we're almost done. Keep still and it will go faster."

Time seemed to slow down. She saw the hair fall to the ground and began to worry. Elizabeth looked out the window and let her mind wander. She thought of sunshine, swings, slides, and sodas.

"Okay, you're all done Elizabeth. What do you think?" asked the woman handing her a mirror.

Elizabeth looked in the mirror and slowly a smile spread across her face. She looked okay. The same girl still looked back at her from the mirror.

"You look great, Lizzie. Now let's get your treat and head to the park. Thank you for being so good," said her mother, taking her hand and helping her off the stool.

1. The story is told from the point of view of

   A. the second person.

   B. the third person.

   C. the first person narrator.

   D. the first person character.

2. Elizabeth's mood at the beginning of the selection is

   A. tense.   B. happy.   C. sad.   D. bored.

3. Short Answer. Use your own paper to write your response. Explain how the character changes by the end of the passage. What causes the change? Use details from the passage to support your answer.

4. The main characters in this passage are Elizabeth and

   A. society.   B. herself.   C. her mother.   D. nature.

5. Short Answer. Use your own paper to write your response. Explain the emotions in the passage. What is Elizabeth struggling against? Use details from the passage to support your answer.

6. Which of the following is Elizabeth's greatest concern in this passage?

    A. Elizabeth is not comfortable sitting still for so long.

    B. Elizabeth is being forced to sit in a time out.

    C. Elizabeth is getting a haircut and is worried about the outcome.

    D. Elizabeth always complains when she has to get a haircut.

7. Which method of characterization is used *most* to reveal the character of Elizabeth?

    A. thought   B. action   C. dialog   D. observation

8. Which of the following is the best statement of theme for this passage?

    A. Fear can be overcome with laughter.

    B. Things can turn out better than expected.

    C. Haircuts are painful.

    D. Good behavior is never rewarded.

Excerpt from *Ethan Frome* by Edith Wharton

I had the story, bit by bit, from various people, and, as generally happens in such cases, each time it was a different story. If you know Starkfield, Massachusetts, you know the post-office. If you know the post-office you must have seen Ethan Frome drive up to it, drop the reins on his hollow-backed bay and drag himself across the brick pavement to the white colonnade: and you must have asked who he was.

It was there that, several years ago, I saw him for the first time; and the sight pulled me up sharp. Even then he was the most striking figure in Starkfield, though he was but the ruin of a man. It was not so much his great height that marked him, for the "natives" were easily singled out by their lank longitude from the stockier foreign breed: it was the careless powerful look he had, in spite of a lameness checking each step like the jerk of a chain. There was something bleak and unapproachable in his face, and he was so stiffened and grizzled that I took him for an old man and was surprised to hear that he was not more than fifty-two. I had this from Harmon Gow, who had driven the stage from Bettsbridge to Starkfield in pre-trolley days and knew the chronicle of all the families on his line.

"He's looked that way ever since he had his smash-up; and that's twenty-four years ago come next February," Harmon threw out between reminiscent pauses.

9. How do we learn about Ethan Frome? Select all that apply.

    A. his actions

    B. his thoughts

    C. his appearance

    D. the comments of others

10. Which is a good description of Ethan Frome?

    A. a strong, powerful man

    B. an old, weak man

    C. a tall, lame man

    D. a quiet, striking man

11. This selection is written *mostly* from what point of view?

    A. first person narrator

    B. second person

    C. third person omniscient

    D. third person limited

12. **Extended Response** Use your own paper to write your response. Write a detailed character description of Ethan Frome. Use details from the selection to support your description. What does Ethan Frome's description tell us about the man?

Chapter 8
Figurative Language in Poetry and Prose

This chapter covers Minnesota Reading Standard(s):

I.D.4 and I.D.7	Students will analyze and evaluate how figurative language and literary devices contribute to the meaning of the text.

POETRY

Poetry is literature written in **lines** and **stanzas**, unlike **prose**, which follows standard grammar rules including sentence and paragraph structure. Also, **rhythm** and **rhyme** often make poetry different from prose. Well-known poets include Robert Frost, Emily Dickinson, and even Shel Silverstein and Dr. Seuss. Most people are familiar with the poem

Roses are Red.

Violets are Blue.

Reading is fun,

and Writing is, too.

Notice that the two words "Blue" and "too" rhyme in this poem.

LITERARY DEVICES

Figurative language is a type of literary device used in both poetry and prose. **Figurative language** is a way of expressing an experience without having to use merely plain, dry facts. Figurative language is not literally true, but it produces creative and powerful descriptions. As an example, think about the phrase, "I couldn't carry a tune in a bucket." No one can really carry a tune in a bucket. And if a tune could be put in a bucket, that person would still have no clue what to do with it. The phrase literally means that a person sings badly off key and out of tune. The expression says the same thing as the true literal phrase but with more feeling and vivid images. Figurative language is a creative and powerful way of using language to express ideas.

Figurative Language in Poetry and Prose

Figurative language gives the reader the opportunity to picture events in poetry and prose in new ways. The types of figurative language are explained below and on the following page. Study the types, and then apply what you learn to the practice passages that follow.

Alliteration: the repetition of consonant sounds at the beginning of words.

> **Example 5:** Grey gorillas greedily gather green grapes.
>
> **Example 6:** "Success is counted sweetest/ By those who ne'er succeed."
>
> > – Emily Dickinson

Hyperbole: an exaggeration or overstating of an idea to create a humorous effect or express a strong emotion.

> **Example 1:** I'm so hungry I could eat a horse.
>
> **Example 2:** In "The Crisis," Thomas Paine describes King George as "a common murderer, a highwayman, or a housebreaker."

Imagery: words and phrases that appeal to the five senses of sight, hearing, touch, smell, or taste. Imagery is often called "word pictures" because a writer recreates an experience for the reader.

> **Example 1:** The aroma of freshly baked cookies filled the kitchen, making my mouth water.
>
> **Example 2:** "Roses, their sharp spines being gone,/ Not royal in their smells alone,/ But in their hue;"
>
> > –Shakespeare

Metaphor: a comparison between two unlike things *without* using the words "like" or "as."

> **Example 1:** Her voice was an angel's song.
>
> **Example 2:** "All the world's a stage,/ And all the men and women merely players"
>
> > – Shakespeare

Onomatopoeia: when a word sounds like what it describes

> **Example 1:** click, hiss, pop, snap
>
> **Example 2:** "There interposed a fly—with blue-uncertain stumbling buzz—"
>
> > – Emily Dickinson

Personification: when an animal or an object is described as if it were human or had human qualities.

> **Example 1:** The stubborn rock refused to be moved.
>
> **Example 2:** "Love's stricken 'Why' is all that love can speak."
>
> > – Emily Dickinson

Rhyme: when words have the same ending sounds.

> **Example 1:** bore/snore, head/bed
>
> **Example 2:** "With spectacles on nose and pouch on side;
> > His youthful hose, well saved, a world too wide"
>
> > – Shakespeare

Rhythm: a pattern of stressed and unstressed syllables in literature. While rhythm is almost always found in poetry, quality prose writing also involves regular patterns that appeal to the reader.

Example 1: We need to hear the sound of laughter.

Example 2: "But soft! What light through yonder window breaks?"
– Shakespeare

Simile: comparison between two things using the words "like" or "as."

Example 1: Happy as a lark.

Example 2: "And then the whining schoolboy, with his satchel/ And shining morning face, creeping like a snail"
– Shakespeare

Practice 1: Figurative Language

Read the following passage. Then, answer the questions about literary devices.

Excerpt from "The Devil and Tom Walker"
by Washington Irving

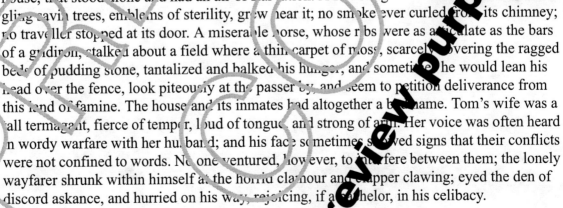

About the year 1727, just at the time when earthquakes were prevalent in New England, and shook many tall sinners down upon their knees, there lived near this place a meagre miserly fellow of the name of Tom Walker. He had a wife as miserly as himself; they were so miserly that they even conspired to cheat each other. Whatever the woman could lay hands on she hid away: a hen could not cackle but she was on the alert to secure the new-laid egg. Her husband was continually prying about to detect her secret hoards, and many and fierce were the conflicts that took place about what ought to have been common property. They lived in a forlorn looking house, that stood alone and had an air of starvation. A few straggling savin trees, emblems of sterility, grew near it; no smoke ever curled from its chimney; no traveller stopped at its door. A miserable horse, whose ribs were as articulate as the bars of a gridiron, stalked about a field where a thin carpet of moss, scarcely covering the ragged beds of pudding stone, tantalized and balked his hunger, and sometimes he would lean his head over the fence, look piteously at the passer by, and seem to petition deliverance from this land of famine. The house and its inmates had altogether a bad name. Tom's wife was a tall termagant, fierce of temper, loud of tongue, and strong of arm. Her voice was often heard in wordy warfare with her husband; and his face sometimes showed signs that their conflicts were not confined to words. No one ventured, however, to interfere between them; the lonely wayfarer shrunk within himself at the horrid clamour and clapper clawing; eyed the den of discord askance, and hurried on his way, rejoicing, if a bachelor, in his celibacy.

Figurative Language in Poetry and Prose

1. Which of the following phrases from the passage is an example of a *simile*?

    A. A few straggling savin trees, emblems of sterility, grew near it;

    B. A miserable horse, whose ribs were as articulate as the bars of a gridiron

    C. They lived in a forlorn looking house, that stood alone and had an air of starvation.

    D. They were so miserly that they even conspired to cheat each other.

2. Which of the following phrases from the passage is an example of *personification*?

    A. A few straggling savin trees, emblems of sterility, grew near it;

    B. A miserable horse, whose ribs were as articulate as the bars of a gridiron

    C. They lived in a forlorn looking house, that stood alone and had an air of starvation.

    D. They were so miserly that they even conspired to cheat each other.

3. Find some examples of *alliteration* in the story.

There is no Frigate like a Book

1 There is no Frigate like a Book
2 To take us Lands away
3 Nor any Coursers like a Page
4 Of prancing Poetry-
5 This Traverse may the poorest take
6 Without oppress of Toll-
7 How frugal is the Chariot
8 That bears the Human soul.

– Emily Dickinson

4. Which of the following lines from the poem contain a *simile*?
    A. line 1   B. line 4   C. line 6   D. line 8

5. Which of the following lines contains an example of a *metaphor*?
    A. lines 1–2   B. lines 3–4   C. lines 5–6   D. lines 7–8

6. Which of the following lines from the poem contain *alliteration*?
    A. lines 1–2   B. lines 3–4   C. lines 5–6   D. lines 7–8

7. Write down the words that *rhyme* in this poem.

---

8. Describe what the *metaphor* from question 5 is comparing.

_____

_____

9. **Short Answer.** Use your own paper to write your response.

   Explain what is being said about books in this poem and how the figurative language helps say it.

Angel

It was just another perfect day in paradise. The sun was just beginning to warm the day, and outside the birds were cheerfully passing along the morning gossip. Looking out my window, I saw a picture postcard: coconut palms in the foreground, silhouetted against a robin's-egg blue sky. I could hear the ocean quietly roaring in the distance, and I felt a sudden urge to feel the white sand under my feet. I walked outside and strolled down our private road to the beach. I walked out onto the sand and looked around; I was happy to see there was no one on the beach. I drew a deep, cleansing breath of sea air and looked up into the sky just in time to see a winged man. Yes, a man with wings swooped down and made a perfect landing in front of me! He stood about six feet tall with longish blonde hair and pale blue eyes. He was wearing faded Levi's and a Hard Rock Cafe tee-shirt. He looked very normal, actually, except for the wings, that is. He was an eagle in jeans. His wings were mostly brown with white tips and must have spanned at least 15 feet across. Before I could begin to recover my senses, he yelled for me to hold on. Crack! There was a blinding flash of light, and I felt my skin ripple. I opened my eyes, and we were sitting in an ornately furnished office. I felt like I had just gotten off the space mountain ride at Disney World. I shook myself in an attempt to clear my head. Where was I? What was going on? I figured I must be dreaming or going insane. Before I could make sense of anything, a door opened on the opposite wall. In walked my high school principal and stood next to the angel. She had that look on her face. Oh no, I was in trouble now. Closing my eyes, I put my head down. I couldn't look her in the face.

"Mr. Johnson? I think you have some explaining to do. Mr. Johnson? Mr. Johnson, I'm talking to you. Mr. Johnson?" she said.

I opened my eyes and saw my English teacher standing over my desk. Rubbing my eyes, I looked around for the angel. What? On my desk in front of me was the short story I had been writing. I must have fallen asleep.

"Mr. Johnson, do you need to go see the principal? There will be no napping in this class," my teacher said.

"I'm sorry, Ms. Ritter. I'll finish my story now," I said. Now I had a really good idea for how to finish it. I think maybe there should be an angel.

10. Write two examples of *onomatopoeia* from this passage.

_____

11. Write an example of *personification* from this passage.

_____

_____

12. Write down a metaphor and a simile from the passage.

_____

_____

_____

13. **Short Answer.** Use your own paper to write your response.

   There are multiple examples of *imagery* in this selection. Write a few examples and explain how they help the story.

Practice 2: Literary Devices

A. **Passage Practice.** Find a favorite poem or short story from your literature book. Read your selection carefully, and locate any figurative language such as metaphors, similes, personification, and hyperbole.

B. **Creative Writing.** Choose a photo or painting that has meaning for you. Write a poem or short story about it using figurative language. Attach the photo or painting to your poem or story.

CHAPTER 8 SUMMARY

- Poetry is literature written in **lines** and **stanzas**.
- Poetry often includes **rhyme** and **rhythm**.
- **Figurative language** conveys ideas and feelings in an imaginative and vivid way.
- Authors use figurative language in both poetry and prose.
- Types of figurative language include **alliteration**, **hyperbole**, **imagry**, **metaphor**, **onomatopoeia**, **personification**, **rhyme**, **rhythm**, and **simile**.

CHAPTER 8 REVIEW

Read the following selections carefully, and then answer the questions.

Excerpt from "The Song of Hiawatha"
by Henry Wadsworth Longfellow

Two good friends had Hiawatha,
Singled out from all the others,
Bound to him in closest union,
And to whom he gave the right hand
Of his heart, in joy and sorrow;
Chibiabos, the musician,
And the very strong man, Kwasind.

Straight between them ran the pathway,
Never grew the grass upon it;
Singing birds, that utter falsehoods,
Story-tellers, mischief-makers,
Found no eager ear to listen,
Could not breed ill-will between them,
For they kept each other's counsel,
Spake with naked hearts together,
Pondering much and much contriving
How the tribes of men might prosper.

Most beloved by Hiawatha
Was the gentle Chibiabos,
He the best of all musicians,
He the sweetest of all singers.
Beautiful and childlike was he,
Brave as man is, soft as woman,
Pliant as a wand of willow,
Stately as a deer with antlers.

When he sang, the village listened;
All the warriors gathered round him,
All the women came to hear him;
Now he stirred their souls to passion,
Now he melted them to pity.

1. What type of literary device is being used in the following quote?

   "And to whom he gave the right hand/Of his heart, in joy and sorrow."

   A. hyperbole   B. imagery   C. rhyme   D. oxymoron

2. What type of literary device is being used in the following quote?

   "Pliant as a wand of willow,/Stately as a deer with antlers."

   A. metaphor   B. simile   C. alliteration   D. symbol

3. What is the figurative language of this phrase, "Now he melted them to pity" saying about Chibiabos' singing?

   A. His magical singing could melt people.

   B. His singing caused people in local villages to pity him.

   C. His singing was awful.

   D. His singing caused them to feel emotion, such as compassion and pity.

The Hitchhike

My grandmother was a truthful woman. She spent her days in honest labor and honorable company. When her children lied to her, they were sent to bed without any supper and with the bitter taste of soap on their tongues. That's why her story must be true. She was 94 when she told it to me, so perhaps time had taken a toll on her senses. Anyway, here is her story, and I'll leave it to you to decide.

It was during World War II, and times were hard. There was never enough money or gas in those days. However, we'd occasionally treat ourselves to a good meal and maybe see a movie too. That night Frank had some business in Glen Flora. That's in Texas, just across the Colorado river. I went with him and decided we would stay in a hotel that night and drive back the next day.

It was sometime in the fall. I remember the cool, crisp air blowing through the window. It was after dusk when we first saw her. I know it was dark because I remember seeing her outline in the lights ahead. There weren't many cars; it was a lonely road. We slowed the car, and the girl stood on the side of the road. We were surprised to see she was dressed in a light, summer dress. She was a pretty, petite thing, about eighteen or nineteen.

"Please take me home, if it's not too far out of your way." Her voice was sweet and somewhat shrill, like the tinkling of bells.

I opened the door and leaned forward. She climbed into the back seat, and we started to drive. Finally, I asked her where she lived.

"Glen Flora." That's all she said at first. It seemed like that one word took all her breath.

"You're in luck. That's just where we're headed," Frank said.

The girl didn't reply. We rode on in silence. I turned around a few times, but the girl just smiled, somewhat sadly. I didn't want to stare at her, but I had questions. Who was she? Why was she walking alone at night?

Just before we got to the river, Frank broke the silence.

"Where is your home, Miss?"

There was no reply.

"Miss? It's beginning to rain, and we can take you home," Frank said.

"Oh," the girl replied. "That would be nice. I live at the corner of Walnut and Live Oak Streets."

"Glen Flora must be a nice place to grow up," I said, but again, there was no reply from the back of the car. I couldn't even hear her breathing. We crossed the bridge, headed into town, and Frank turned onto Walnut Street. As we pulled up before the shuttered house, we turned around to say goodbye. The back seat was empty!

"Where did she go?" Frank asked. "She wouldn't have just jumped out, would she?"

There had to be some explanation. We hurried toward the house. We rang insistently on the doorbell. A gray-haired man opened the door.

"Excuse me," Frank said, "but the strangest thing has just happened. We picked up your daughter from the side of the road, but she seems to have disappeared."

"Yes, yes, I know," said the man wearily. "This has happened several times in the past months. My daughter was killed in an automobile accident almost two years ago..."

Grandma went on to tell me that after getting over the shock, they realized what had happened. They had had a ghost in their back seat. The proof, she said, was that a ghost can not cross water. That was why, when they came to the river, the girl had only one choice: to disappear!

4. What type of literary device is being used in the following quote?

   "Her voice was sweet and somewhat shrill, like the tinkling of bells."

   A. personification   B. oxymoron   C. simile   D. metaphor

5. What type of figurative language is being used in the following quote?

   "They were sent to bed without any supper and with the bitter taste of soap on their tongues."

   A. imagery   B. metaphor   C. personification   D. hyperbole

6. What type of figurative language is being used in the following quote?

   "It seemed like that one word took all her breath."

   A. imagery   B. onomatopoeia   C. metaphor   D. hyperbole

7. Find an example of *imagery* in the selection.

Figurative Language in Poetry and Prose

White Water

Sprayed by clear, cool water, you wonder if the bow of the rubber raft will rise enough to clear the raging rapids ahead. Whoosh! It does, although the raft bends between the white water. The boatman skillfully guides it around the bulging boulders. This is one of the thrills of floating the Peshtigo River in the Wisconsin Northwoods. Each of the rapids presents a special navigation problem, so the guide's experience, knowledge, and skillful strong arms serve to keep the boat off the rocks and you out of the water. Most people who float the river arrange for an outfitter to provide everything, so you have the option of sitting back and enjoying the ride, at least until the next wave of white water washes over you. The biggest thrill comes at Rock Slide Rapid, a class 3 – 4 rapid. Once you pass these, you might like to take a turn with the oars, but soon your shoulders will scream for a break. Listen to them. Listen to the soothing sounds of the river. Let yourself float like a leaf. The trip is constantly changing landscape. When you finally reach the end, you will be thrilled and exhausted.

8. Write an example of *onomatopoeia* from this passage.

_____

9. Write an example of *personification* from this passage.

_____

10. Write an example of *alliteration* from this passage.

_____

11. Write an example of a *simile* from the passage "White Water."

_____

Excerpt from "The Raven"
by Edgar Allen Poe

Once upon a midnight dreary, while I pondered, weak and weary,	1
Over many a quaint and curious volume of forgotten lore—	2
While I nodded, nearly napping, suddenly there came a tapping,	3
As of someone gently rapping, rapping at my chamber door—	4
"'Tis some visitor," I muttered "tapping at my chamber door—	5
Only this and nothing more."	6
Ah, distinctly I remember it was in the bleak December	7
And each separate dying ember wrought its ghost upon the floor.	8
Eagerly I wished the morrow;—vainly I had sought to borrow	9
From my books surcease of sorrow—sorrow for the lost Lenore—	10
For the rare and radiant maiden whom the angels name the Lenore—	11
Nameless here for evermore.	12

And the silken sad uncertain rustling of each purple curtain 13
Thrilled me—filled me with fantastic terrors never felt before; 14
So that now, to still the beating of my heart, I stood repeating 15
"'Tis some visitor entreating entrance at my chamber door; 16
Some late visitor entreating entrance at my chamber door 17
This it is and nothing more 18

Presently my soul grew stronger; hesitating then no longer, 19
"Sir," said I, "or Madam, truly your forgiveness I implore; 20
But the fact is I was napping, and so gently you came rapping, 21
And so faintly you came tapping, tapping at my chamber door, 22
That I scarce was sure I heard you"—here I opened wide the door,— 23
Darkness there and nothing more. 24

12. Which one of the following lines from the poem contains *personification*?

    A. line 1   B. line 7   C. line 13   D. line 20

13. Which one of the following lines contains an example of *alliteration*?

    A. line 1   B. line 5   C. line 15   D. line 17

14. Write down some of the words that *rhyme* in this poem.

_____

15. Find two examples of onomatopoeia.

_____

16. **Extended Response** Use your own paper to write your response.

    How did this poem affect you? Explain.

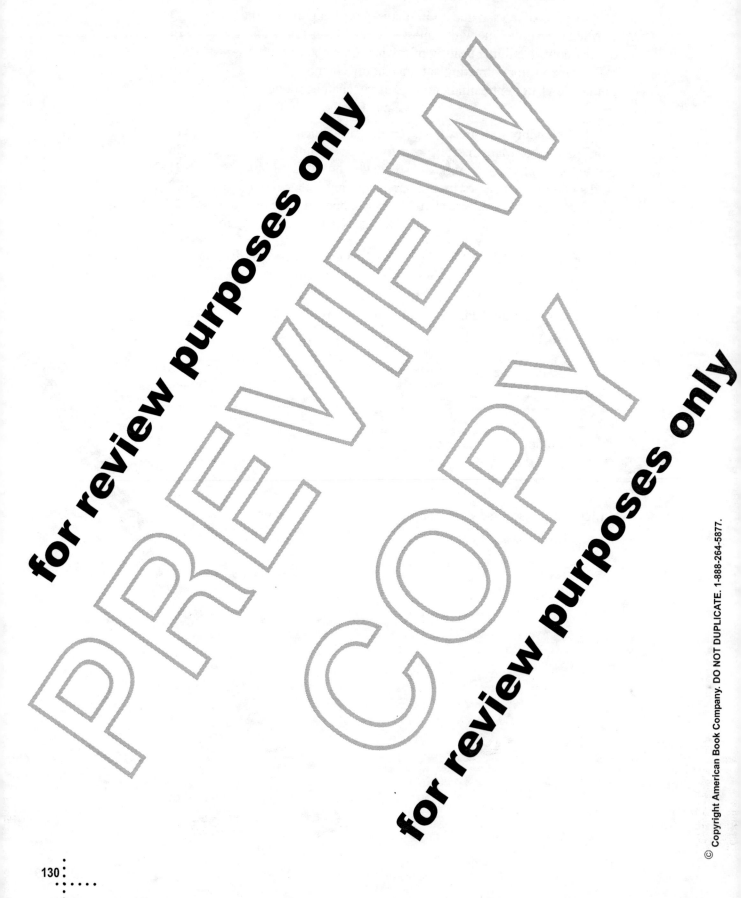

Chapter 9
Writing the Constructed Response

This chapter covers Minnesota Reading Standard(s):

I.D.4 and I.D.7	Students will analyze and evaluate how figurative language and literary devices contribute to the meaning of the text.

For some items on the MCA-II Grade 8 Reading Test, you are asked to read and write about different passages, both fiction and nonfiction texts. Items emphasize the important understandings you are expected to gain from reading, and you will base your written responses on the reading passage.

The constructed-response items should be read very carefully. These items will let you know what is expected of you. The test directions will also say that questions must be answered using information from the passage, *not* prior knowledge.

Trained readers score responses to questions based on state-adopted **rubrics**, which are scales that describe different levels of performance. The trained readers follow scoring procedures that have been developed to ensure a high degree of objectivity and reliability. Before we learn to write a **constructed response**, let's take a look at the general scoring rubrics for a constructed response.

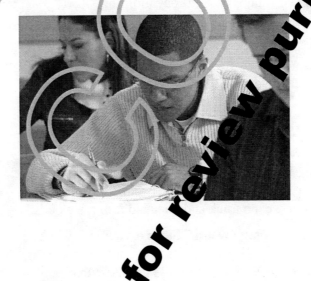

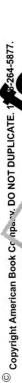

SCORING RUBRICS FOR A CONSTRUCTED RESPONSE

4-POINT GENERAL RUBRIC FOR CONSTRUCTED-RESPONSE ITEMS

4 pts   The response indicates that the student has a thorough understanding of the reading concept asked for in the task. The student has provided a response that is accurate, complete, and fulfills all the requirements of the task. Necessary support and/or examples are included, and the information is clearly text-based.

3 pts   The response indicates that the student has an understanding of the reading concept asked for in the task. The student has provided a response that is accurate and fulfills all the requirements of the task, but the required support and/or details are not complete or clearly text-based.

2 pts   The response indicates that the student has a partial understanding of the reading concept asked for in the task. The student has provided a response that includes information that is essentially correct and text-based, but the information is too general or too simplistic. Some of the support and/or examples and requirements of the task may be incomplete or omitted.

1 pt   The response indicates that the student has very limited understanding of the reading concept asked for in the task. The response is incomplete, may exhibit many flaws, and may not address all the requirements of the task.

0 pts   The response is inaccurate, confused, and/or irrelevant, or the student has failed to respond to the task.

Now, read the following selection. Then, on page, study how a student replied to an extended-response question. This sample reply would be a model response, and the test graders would likely assign the highest point value (4) to this response.

Life Is but a Dream

Steve got up one Saturday morning, barely awake. He stumbled into the kitchen and grabbed some orange juice. His roommate, Jeff, came in a little later.

"Man, that was a strange dream I had last night," Jeff yawned sleepily.

"What did you dream, Jeff?" Steve asked.

"Well, I dreamed that you and I were at a gas station. We found some fire hoses and were dousing each other with water. Then, you jumped into your pickup truck and wrecked it in the woods."

"That's pretty weird," Steve muttered. "You know, I had a similar dream last night. Only, in my dream, I was driving my truck and it slipped and spun out of control on a patch of ice. It was probably that junk food we ate last night."

Just then, the phone rang. Jeff picked it up. "Hello," he said.

"Hi, is this Steve?" the woman asked.

"Just a second," Jeff said and handed the phone to Steve.

"Hello," Steve answered.

"Hi, my name is Allison. I work with your girlfriend, Jenny. She just twisted her ankle and wants to know if you can pick her up."

"OK. Tell her I'll be right here," Steve said. "I'm on my way now." After he hung up, Steve told Jeff what had happened and jumped in his truck.

"Rats," Steve griped aloud, "I'm almost out of gas." He pulled into a gas station near his apartment and fueled up. After paying the attendant, Steve drove onto the road. It was a four-lane road with no divider lane. It was raining, so he had to drive carefully. Driving in the left lane, Steve suddenly had to slam on his brakes, as the car in front of him was stopping to make a left turn. The truck began to skid forward. Quickly, Steve turned the wheel to the right. Because he was hydroplaning, the truck went to the left instead of to the right, directly into oncoming traffic. Steve braced himself as he hit a smaller truck in a head-on collision. Steve opened his eyes in shock at the scene before him. His truck was bashed in past the radiator. Luckily, Steve was wearing his seat belt and was unhurt. The truck Steve hit was smashed in to the engine, and the engine was on fire. Steve helped the driver out of his burning vehicle.

The driver in this car was also unhurt because his airbag had opened. The police came, and the fire trucks were called in to put out the fire. Totally freaked out, Steve called Jeff back at the apartment from a pay phone.

"Jeff," he said shakily, "I think that maybe you were supposed to pick up my girlfriend, Jenny, today . . ."

The constructed-response question on the MCA-II Grade 8 Reading Test might read as follows:

> Write a constructed-response describing the two dreams in this selection. Explain how each dreaming character reacts to the dream the way he does. Use details and examples from the selection to support your ideas.

MODEL STUDENT RESPONSE: 4 POINT SCORE

The two characters, Jeff and Steve, in "Life Is but a Dream" both have dreams concerning an accident involving Steve's truck. In Jeff's dream, there is comic relief of playing with fire hoses before Steve jumps in his truck and wrecks it. He does not take the dream seriously or see danger ahead for Steve's life. In Steve's dream, he is driving his truck when he loses control on a patch of ice. Steve does not take the dream seriously either, and he immediately attributes it to the junk food they ate the night before. Neither is alarmed by the dream, nor is there any foreboding sense of danger. After Steve wrecks his truck, he is aware that maybe he was not supposed to pick up his girlfriend, and just maybe his dream had substance after all. Sometimes we should not dismiss things just because they may be painful.

Scoring Rubric: 4 Points

4 pts The response states that the dreaming characters have one thing in common: they do their best to block out painful ideas and go after more pleasant ones. The response gives a reason for dismissing the dream is the junk food as its reason. The unpleasantness of the dream, or even facing the fact that there might be some meaning or warning in the dream is not something that either one is willing to face at the time. In dismissing the dream, they both can go on with their lives as if nothing has happened. Only after Steve's wreck can they put substance or validity to the dreams. We are more likely to dismiss dreams if they don't make us feel good.

Annotation: 4 Points

The response correctly addresses all aspects of the item; the student correctly explains each character's dream and how he reacts to the dream. The student uses sufficient details and information from the selection to support the response.

Read the selection on the following page. Then study how a student replied to a constructed-response question. The sample response would be a model answer, and the test graders would likely assign a 3-point value to this response.

I Dreamt . . .

I dreamt last night that we had parted.
We strolled no longer through the lane.
No nightingale its trilling started
In gardens sear–all life was pain

My misery like a cloud above me
Deprived my soul of laughter's lilt
I asked, "Why does my love not love me?
In what, O love, consists my guilt?"
My tortured thoughts were turbid, sickly.
To questions there was no reply.
How could her fancy change so quickly?
How could such love abate and die?

I woke to memories reassuring,
For yesterday, to my great pride,
I heard sweet words of love, ensuring
That you will never leave my side.

To die a little, parting seems,
So let us only part in dreams

– Suleiman Rustam

The constructed-response question on the MCA-II Grade 8 Reading Test might read as follows:

In a constructed-response, evaluate the troubled nature of the narrator of this poem and explain four results or consequences of his dream.

MODEL STUDENT RESPONSE - 3 POINT SCORE

In "I Dreamt . . ." the poet has a dream that is actually a nightmare. His greatest fear becomes a reality in the dream. The speaker has lost the loved one who made life worth living. They no longer are strolling the garden lanes together. A cloud of darkness hangs over the speaker's head. But, when the poet awakens, he immediately hears in his heart the words of his sweetheart from the day before. The words assure him of her undying love for him and that they will never part. The poet is relieved that the dream is not reality.

SCORING RUBRIC: 3 POINTS

3 pts   The response states that the poet has a nightmare, and he is troubled. The response may also state that the activities that he and his love do together are no longer done. All life is pain for him. He feels misery like a cloud over him, and his heart is no longer able to laugh and sing. In his state of trouble, he is sick at heart. He questions why his love no longer cares for him. When he awakens, he is able to distinguish the dream from reality, and immediately responds in his heart to the words of love spoken the previous day by his sweetheart that she will never leave his side.

Annotation: 3 Points

The student identifies and explains the dream and states that the poet is tortured in his thoughts over what he has done to lose this love in his life. The student's response is less thorough than a 4-point response in stating how troubled the poet is in his dream. The student does address and explain four results or consequences of his dream.

Practice 1:   Reviewing the Sample Response

Now that you have read the sample constructed-responses, take a moment to notice which facts and details from the passages were in some way used when writing the responses. Discuss these with your teacher.

Practice 2:   Writing a Constructed-Response

Read the following stories. Make note of the details of the stories, and then answer the extended-response question that follows each story.

A Soldier's Lesson

It was in the sixth week of basic training, and I was getting quite tired during our mock battlefield training exercise. After a six-mile march in full gear, we had to dig our foxholes (underground defensive positions) and settle in for the night. The afternoon sun was beating hard, and we had to dig with a very small shovel known as an entrenching tool.

As we dug, my ranger buddy (person who works with you as a team), Private Nixen, turned to me and said, "Hey Regis! We need branches to camouflage our foxhole. Why don't you go get them?"

"Sure," I answered. "As long as you can watch my M16. You know how the enemy unit is always trying to outwit us. They may try to steal it from me as I gather wood."

"No problem," Nixen said.

Private Bryant, who was within earshot of our foxhole, shouted, "Be careful out there—you never know when the enemy is going to strike."

So, off I went to gather branches loaded with leaves. This task took longer than I expected. It took me almost thirty minutes to get to camp. However, when I returned, I would wish I had stayed away.

My Drill Sergeant, Oglethorpe, was standing next to Nixen and had a look that would melt mountains. He thundered, "Private, do you know where your M16 is? Do you?"

"Drill Sergeant, I-I don't know where it is," I stammered. I looked over at my ranger buddy, but Nixen remained silent.

"Well, the enemy unit returned it to me. They said they had found the rifle unattended, and so they took it. Do you have any idea how embarrassing that is to me?" Oglethorpe growled through clenched teeth.

"It is my fault," I tried to reply with dignity. "I know, ultimately, the rifle is my responsibility." Once I said this, my drill sergeant shared some unsavory words with me, ordered me to hold my rifle in front of me for thirty minutes, and stomped off. My arms grew very sore during this exercise. The next day, Friday, the platoon returned to the barracks. Everyone was allowed to go off-post Friday and Saturday on leave and return Sunday. Unfortunately, I was not permitted to leave the barracks for the weekend. Because of the loss of my rifle, I had to stay behind and clean the latrines in my barracks. However, I suffered through this and just considered it one of life's memorable experiences. I still remember Nixen's look of relief and happiness when he left for his two-day leave.

– Dick Rags

1. **Constructed-Response.** Use your own paper to write your response.

The lead character in the story makes the decision not to tell the truth. Describe the decision the private makes, and explain the circumstances that help create that decision.

The Tortoise and the Eagle

It was not often that the tortoise and the eagle met, for the one spent his days in the clouds and the other under a bush. However, when the eagle heard what a warm-hearted little fellow the tortoise was, he went to pay a call on him. The tortoise family showed such pleasure in his company and fed him so lavishly that the eagle returned again and again, while every time as he flew away he laughed, 'Ha ha! I can enjoy the hospitality of the tortoise on the ground, but he can never reach my eyrie in the treetop!"

The eagle's frequent visits, his selfishness, and ingratitude became the talk of the forest animals. The eagle and the frog were never on speaking terms, for the eagle was accustomed to swooping down to carry a frog home for supper. So the frog called from the stream bank, "Friend tortoise, give me beans, and I will give you wisdom." After enjoying the bowl of beans, the frog said, "Friend tortoise, the eagle is abusing your kindness, for after every visit he flies away laughing, 'Ha ha!

I can enjoy the hospitality of the tortoise on the ground, but he can never enjoy mine, for my eyrie is in the treetops!' Next time the eagle visits you, say, 'Give me a gourd, and I will send food to your wife and children too.'"

The eagle did as the tortoise suggested. He brought a gourd, enjoyed a feast, and as he left he called back, "I will call later for the present for my wife." The eagle flew away laughing to himself as usual, "Ha ha! I have enjoyed the tortoise's food, but he can never come to my eyrie to taste of mine."

The frog arrived and said, "Now, tortoise, get into the gourd. Your wife will cover you over with fresh food, and the eagle will carry you to his home in the treetops." Presently, the eagle returned.

The tortoise's wife told him, "My husband is away, but he left this gourd filled with food for your family."

The eagle flew away with the gourd, little suspecting that the tortoise was inside. The tortoise could hear every word as the eagle laughed, "Ha! ha! I share the tortoise's food, but he can never visit my eyrie to share mine."

As the gourd was emptied out onto the eagle's eyrie, the tortoise crawled from it and said, "Friend eagle, you have so often visited my home that I thought it would be nice to enjoy the hospitality of yours."

The eagle was furious. "I will peck the flesh from your bones," he said. But he only hurt his beak against the tortoise's hard back.

"I see what sort of friendship you offer me," said the tortoise, "when you threaten to tear me limb from limb." He continued, "Under the circumstances, please take me home, for our pact of friendship is at an end."

"Take you home, indeed!" shrieked the eagle. "I will fling you to the ground and you will be smashed to bits in your fall."

The tortoise bit hold of the eagle's leg. "Let me go, let go of my leg, let go of my leg," groaned the great bird.

"I will gladly do so when you set me down at my own home," mumbled the tortoise through feathers, and he tightened his hold on the eagle's leg.

The eagle flew high into the clouds and darted down with the speed of an arrow. He shook his leg. He turned and twirled, but it was to no use. He could not rid himself of the tortoise until he set him down safely in his own home. As the eagle flew away the tortoise called after him, "Friendship requires the contribution of two parties. For example, I welcome you, and you welcome me. Since, however, you have chosen to make a mockery of it, laughing at me for my hospitality, you need not call again."

The End

Courtesy of the *AFRO-American Almanac*

2. **Constructed-Response.** Use your own paper to write your response.

Describe the action the tortoise took in this story. Explain why he decides to take that action and how it influences his life. Use four details and examples from the selection to support your ideas.

CHAPTER 9 SUMMARY

- **Constructed-Response items** should be read very carefully. These items will let you know what is expected of you. The test directions will also indicate that questions must be answered using information from the passage, *not* prior knowledge.

- Points are assigned based on a **4 point scale** beginning with the highest point value possible, 4, and on down to 0, the lowest point value possible.

- **Trained readers** will follow these scoring procedures while evaluating each of your three constructed-responses.

- You will write your constructed responses on **special pages** of the test consisting of about 18 lines.

CHAPTER 9 REVIEW

Read the following passages, and answer the constructed-response question at the end of each.

Seize the Day!

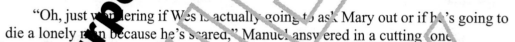

I sat down at the lunch table and told my friend, Manuel, a junior, about my latest crush. "Man, I hope she likes me. She's just so beautiful. I mean, I really like her, but I'm afraid I'm not popular enough for her."

"Stop it, Wes," Manuel said. "So you're not the best looking guy in the school. You still have a chance—you just have to talk to her."

"Hey guys, what's up?" Tad asked as he took a seat next to Manuel and me at the lunch table.

"Oh, just wondering if Wes is actually going to ask Mary out or if he's going to die a lonely man because he's scared," Manuel answered in a cutting tone.

"Come on!" Tad urged. "You can do it! Now, get up there and talk to her like a normal human being!"

"I can't," I mumbled. "I don't want to be the joke of the school."

"Fine. Then, I'll be the joke!" Manuel stated firmly. "Two months of this kind of talk is long enough!" Manuel got up from the table and walked to where Mary was standing in line. I could hear him clearly.

"Hi, Mary, how are you doing?" Manuel asked with a grin.

"Fine," Mary replied as she looked him straight in the eyes, her long hair streaming down her face.

"Hey, Mary—I was wondering," Manuel began, "two of my friends are meeting their dates at this special club for teens called *Latin Flavors*. I was wondering if you would like to join me—they have free salsa and merengue dance classes there on Fridays." At this point, even Manuel's voice started cracking nervously.

"Well . . . I'd love to," Mary smiled gently as she answered.

"Ok," Manuel said, relieved. "Could I have your number so we can arrange when to meet at the club?"

"Sure," Mary nodded. "Oh, by the way, tell your friend Wes, hi."

"You got it," Manuel said. "See you Friday." He walked quickly back to the lunch table.

I was getting really upset with this turn of events, but I just faked a smile and asked, "So, how did it go?"

"Well, you're now looking at the man who's got a date with Mary!"

"Good job," I muttered uneasily.

"Oh, by the way, Wes, Mary says, hi," Manuel said, digging his elbow into my stomach. I got a lump in my throat that wouldn't go away . . .

Seven years later, I was the best man at the wedding of Mary and Manuel. At the outdoor reception, Mary walked up to me and straight out said, "You know, I had the biggest crush on you in high school. I guess you were after someone else."

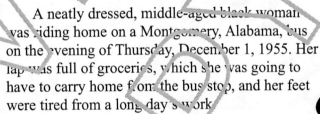

"There was no one else," I confessed while looking down at the grass.

"Well," sighed Mary as she filled up two glasses of punch, one for me and one for herself, "here's to 'what if?'" Our glasses clinked together as Mary chuckled ruefully. I spilled part of the drink as I realized how much my shyness may have cost me . . .

1. **Constructed-Response** Use your own paper to write your response.

To what extent are Wes' feelings about himself responsible for his decision not to talk to Mary? Explain and give some results of this decision.

Rosa Parks Wouldn't Budge

A neatly dressed, middle-aged black woman was riding home on a Montgomery, Alabama, bus on the evening of Thursday, December 1, 1955. Her lap was full of groceries, which she was going to have to carry home from the bus stop, and her feet were tired from a long day's work.

Mrs. Rosa Parks was sitting in the first row of seats behind the section marked "Whites Only." When she chose this seat, there had been plenty of empty ones both in front of and behind the "Great Divide." Now they were occupied, and black passengers were standing in the aisle at the rear.

Then two white men got aboard. They dropped their dimes into the fare box. The driver called over his shoulder, "Niggers move back." Three of the passengers obediently rose from their seats in the black section and stood in the aisle. Rosa Parks did not.

Even when the driver repeated his order and heads turned to see who was "making trouble," she sat as if she hadn't heard. The driver swore under his breath, pulled over to the curb, put on the brakes, and came to stand above her.

"I said to move back. You hear?"

All conversation stopped. No one dared move. Mrs. Parks continued to stare out the window at the darkness. The driver waited. Sounds of other traffic dramatized the silence in the bus.

It was a historic moment: the birth of a movement that was to challenge and ultimately change the social patterns that had established themselves in most Americans' minds as a way of life which was traditional and deeply rooted in the South.

Actually, that tradition of racial segregation—loosely nicknamed Jim Crow—was not as venerable as most of its adherents believed. Many segregation laws, especially those concerned with public transportation, only dated from the turn of the twentieth century and at the start had been resisted, through boycotts, by Southern blacks, sometimes successfully.

2. **Constructed-Response.** Use your own paper to write your response.

Rosa Parks refused to give up her seat on the bus. Explain two reasons for her action. With details from this passage, describe two effects that her action had on those around her at that time.

Chapter 10
Comparing and Contrasting

This chapter covers Minnesota Reading Standard(s):

I.D.12	Students will respond to literature using ideas from the text to support reactions and make literary connections.

Comparing and **contrasting** is the process of looking for similarities and differences between two or more objects, characters, or ideas. On the MCA-II Grade 8 Reading Test, you will be required to read a literary passage. Then you may be asked to react and compare characters, purposes, arguments, or messages in two passages. You may also be asked to write responses in which you compare and contrast ideas, characters, or situations in two reading passages.

In this chapter, you will learn about comparing and contrasting as a reading as well as a writing skill. You will also practice answering questions about comparing and contrasting.

INTRODUCTION TO COMPARING AND CONTRASTING

One of the most important aspects of comparing and contrasting is to look for similarities or differences within the same category. A familiar way to express this idea is to make sure you are comparing "apples to apples" and "oranges to oranges" but not "apples to oranges." For example, consider the following sentence:

This candy is tangy and sweet, but that candy is green.

This statement compares flavor and color which are two unrelated categories. We may be able to conclude that the writer likes sweet candy and does not like green candy, but we can't adequately compare the two candies because we don't know the color of the sweet candy, and we don't know the flavor of the green candy. Therefore, when comparing and contrasting two things or ideas, stay in the same category.

2004 © Copyright American Book Company. DO NOT DUPLICATE. 1-888-264-5877.

COMPARING AND CONTRASTING IN A READING PASSAGE

Sometimes, finding similarities and differences that are described in a reading passage can be difficult. Two strategies that can help you with comparing and contrasting are the following:

- Looking for signal words
- Creating an H-map

As you review a reading passage in order to answer questions about comparing and contrasting, you can look for **signal words** that point to a similarity or a difference in the selection. Studying the following list of signal words will help you find similarities and differences in reading passages.

Signal Words for Similarities and Differences			
Similarities		**Differences**	
again	too	although	not as / not like
also	as well as	but	on the contrary
both	just as ... so too	contrary to	on the other hand
likewise	the same	despite	neither
once more		different from	regardless
similarly		even though	still
similar to		however	though
in the same way		in contrast	yet
like		in opposition	unlike
as		in spite of	whereas
in a related way		instead	while
parallel		nevertheless	conversely

Read the following passage which compares the United States (US) and the Union of Soviet Socialist Republics (USSR) regarding their involvement in World War II and the Cold War. As you read, notice the bolded signal words that point to similarities or differences.

Neither the United States nor the USSR had wanted to enter World War II. **Both** had been forced to enter the fighting because of sneak attacks. The Soviets were caught off guard when Hitler broke his non-aggression treaty and invaded the Soviet Union on June 22, 1941. **Similarly**, the United States suffered a surprise attack when the Japanese struck the US naval base at Pearl Harbor on December 7, 1941. From that time on, the two countries were allies in fighting the Axis powers of Germany, Italy, and Japan.

Both countries, **however**, had very different ideological systems. The United States had long prided itself as a strong democracy with an emphasis on free enterprise. **In contrast**, the Soviet Union was **still** under the strict one-party rule of the Communists, who exercised strict government control over the economy. The United States contributed vast amounts of hardware and technical superiority to the war effort **but** relatively few soldiers. **On the other hand**, the Soviets provided very little technical development **but** millions of soldiers. The Soviets lost over 20 million lives in the war, **while** 290,000 US soldiers were killed in World War II.

After the defeat of their common enemy, the US and the USSR battled over their ideological differences. The United States pushed for free elections and open markets, **while** the Soviets wanted "friendly" Communist governments installed in formerly occupied territories. During this conflict called the Cold War, **both** countries tried to use economic and political means to exert influence in different parts of the world. **Likewise**, **both** countries tried to gain superiority in the development of nuclear weapons.

After using signal words to identify similarities and differences, you can clarify your findings by **creating an H-map**. An H-map is a simple diagram shaped like the letter H. In the bridge of the H, you list the similarities, and in each column of the H, you list the differences. Make sure you label each column with the key concept you are comparing and contrasting.

Below is an example of a completed H-map based on the reading passage from the previous page. It shows the similarities and differences between the US and the USSR during World War II and the Cold War.

Differences US	Cold War Similarities	Differences USSR
• attacked by Japan • democracy • free enterprise • contributed hardware and technical superiority • relatively few soldiers killed: 290,000 • in Cold War, pushed for free elections and open markets in many countries	• didn't want to enter WWII • forced into fighting by sneak attacks • allies against the Axis powers • used political and economic means to exert influence in other countries during Cold War • competed in nuclear arms race	• attacked by Germany • strict one-party Communist rule • government controlled economy • few technical contributions to war • contributed millions of soldiers' lives: 20 million lives lost • wanted friendly Communist governments installed in former territories

Practice 1: Comparing and Contrasting in a Passage

Read the following passage. Underline the signal words that indicate similarities or differences. Then create an H-map which highlights the similarities and differences between the French and English colonization of North America.

The main interest of 17th century French colonizers in North America was trade in animal furs. Some furs were used for hats that were very popular in France at the time. The Native Americans were valuable trading partners to the French, supplying animal pelts from beaver, otter, muskrat and mink. Consequently, the French saw no need to try to conquer them. Likewise, the French did not destroy the forests because they wanted to maintain the habitat of the animals they valued so much. Because the northern areas of North America, where the French colonized, were sparsely populated, epidemics took less of a toll. Similarly, the French tended to see native peoples as equals, and they accepted intermarriage. The Native Americans were also valuable to the French as allies in wars against the British.

In contrast, the English colonies may be called "colonies of settlement" where settlers tried to establish English society in the New World. They took control of the land and brought their own political and economic systems, as well as crops and animals. The English came to the New World in much greater numbers than the French, and they wanted control of more and more land, thus displacing great numbers of Native Americans. The Native Americans were not as beneficial economically to the English as to the French, so the English saw them, instead, as an obstacle to progress and a nuisance.

COMPARING AND CONTRASTING ARGUMENTS

In this section, you will learn how to compare and contrast opposing arguments in two reading selections.

An **argument** is a method of logic or reasoning that persuades an audience to accept a certain position on an issue. A writer uses **reasons**, **examples**, or **evidence** to support an argument. Often, you will read arguments that support directly opposite positions regarding all sorts of issues. As a skillful reader, you need not be swayed by every argument that you encounter. Skillful reading requires you to

- analyze the support for each argument;
- evaluate the validity of each position; and
- compare and contrast opposing arguments.

Then, you can take a stand on the most convincing argument. As an example, read the following two opposing viewpoints on capital punishment. How do the arguments differ?

> To the Editor:
>
> I'm outraged that the governor of Illinois has recently placed a moratorium executions in his state. The legal process for capital punishment already takes too long. Some people say that execution isn't a deterrent, but I think that's because there's too much time between the crime and the punishment. The appeals can drag on for 20 years.
>
> Violent crime in this country is becoming more and more of a problem. Some people commit such terrible acts of violence that they can never be rehabilitated. They must be eliminated. How can we stand by and do nothing when a person commits such a horrible crime as multiple murders? It's outrageous! Our inaction makes us just as barbaric as the criminal.
>
> Murder is a terrible thing no matter who's doing it. But if we don't hold on to "an eye for an eye," the whole society will break down into lawlessness. Capital punishment may not be the best way, but it's the best we've got. We can't be afraid to use it, or I'm afraid what the consequences might be.
>
> Sincerely,
>
> *Alex Caldwell*
>
> Alex Caldwell

To the Editor:

I want to applaud the governor of Illinois for his recent decision to stop all executions in his state until further review of the capital punishment system. Contrary to popular belief, capital punishment is not a deterrent to crime. In fact, statistics show that states without capital punishment have a lower rate of violent crime: 3.6 murders per 100,000 persons. States with capital punishment have a higher rate of violent crime: 5.5 murders per 100,000 persons. Other people claim that the appeals process takes too long. However, the Death Penalty Information Center reports that 21 condemned inmates have been released from death row since 1993, including seven from the state of Illinois. We cannot risk the execution of innocent people by speeding up the appeals process. Even the American Bar Association of lawyers has called for a temporary halt to all executions. The system is terribly flawed, and we must stop all executions before other innocent people are killed.

Murder is wrong, no matter who does it, whether it is the state or a convicted criminal. In other words, "Why do we kill people who kill people to show that killing people is wrong?" I hope that other states follow the lead of Illinois and stop all executions. Perhaps this will be a first step in breaking the cycle of violence that holds our country in its grip.

Sincerely,

Felisha Nelson

Felisha Nelson

Obviously, Alex Caldwell supports capital punishment, while Felisha Nelson opposes it. Both writers are convinced of their positions and convey their arguments with reasonable and determined language. They also use a relatively formal tone which is appropriate for a letter to the editor. To analyze arguments, you must look beneath the language and tone to the reasons, examples, and evidence that support each argument. The first step in this process is to make a chart, like the one below, that lists the claims of each side regarding a particular issue.

Capital Punishment:	
Arguments for - Alex Caldwell	**Arguments Against - Felisha Nelson**
1. Executions reduce crime.	1. No executions reduce crime.
2. Lengthy appeals delay punishment.	2. Lengthy appeals prevent the execution of innocent people.
3. Execution of convicted criminals is justified: an eye for an eye, a tooth for a tooth.	3. Execution of convicted criminals is still murder and sends a mixed message to citizens.
4. Capital punishment prevents lawlessness and violence.	4. Capital punishment should be abolished because violence creates violence.

Comparing and Contrasting

Once you know the claims of each side, you must look at the support for each of these claims. In the chart above, claims 1 and 2 can be evaluated in terms of verifiable evidence. Felisha Nelson uses statistics to show that states that execute criminals have higher rates of violent crime. She also shows that, since 1993, the lengthy appeals process has prevented 21 people from being wrongly executed. Alex Caldwell offers no support for his claims. Claims 3 and 4 are offered by both authors as a matter of educated opinion. You must determine their validity on your own. The following paragraph is an example of how one student responded to these arguments in two different reading selections.

Stop Capital Punishment!

Having read both of their arguments, I would have to agree with Felisha Nelson. Capital punishment should be stopped. Executions do not reduce crime, there is always a danger of executing innocent people, and violent acts create more violent acts. Mr. Caldwell says that executions reduce crime, but he lacks any evidence for his argument other than his own opinion about the issue. On the other hand, Ms. Nelson not only states that executions do not reduce crime, but she also points to statistics that show that states without capital punishment actually have a lower violent crime rate.

Practice 2: Compare and Contrast Arguments

A. Capital Punishment

Review the arguments presented above in "Stop Capital Punishment!" Answer the following questions on a separate sheet of paper:

1. Do you agree that Felisha Nelson's argument is more convincing? Why or why not?

2. What is your opinion about capital punishment? Make a list of reasons why you agree or disagree with Felisha Nelson's position. Then write a paragraph in which you argue your position. Also, be sure to mention within the paragraph why you think the opposing view is wrong.

B. Television in Schools

Read the following two letters to the editor on the issue of having televisions in the classroom. Then, respond to the questions that follow.

To the Editor,

It seems to me that there is no sanctuary to turn to, no safe place to go, no place to hide from the scourge of our society — television. Not even our schools are to be held pure from its corroding influence. Despite all the publicity about TV and the national studies that have been done which show a bitter harvest of lower grades, obesity, immaturity, violent role modeling, and a certain level of callousness to the suffering of others, we are fed a steady diet of television.

There are televisions in restaurants, sports arenas, break rooms at work, and every hospital room. In each of these places where television has been introduced, there is a gain by the businesses which install it: people eat more, drink more, interact less, serve people less, and generally cause less work and worry for the estab-

148

lishment. But ask yourself, what do the people really gain? A sterile, impersonal environment, that's what. Is this what we want in our schools? Whether or not we do, television is being embraced by our schools.

What do the schools have to gain? They say that Channel Two and a Half, Public Domain TV, and other stations are useful tools in education: taking kids on visual journeys around the world, teaching foreign languages, and even illustrating government sanctioned value systems. Sure. But any good book, a class of motivated students, and a fine teacher can achieve the same results and often better since the students would be actively engaged in the learning process, instead of being passively attached to the electronic pacifier.

Television has often been portrayed as a drug, and rightly so. Remember that the first generation which was exposed to mind-rotting sitcoms and violent cartoons was the baby boom generation. After being raised on altered reality, they adopted the anti-social philosophy of "tune in and drop out." Does anyone really think that it is only coincidental that "tuning in" refers both to drugs and television: each creates an altered state.

In conclusion, as a 17-year-old high school student, I'm simply tired of having this despicable stone in my face, 24/7. There is a great kids' book my brother got from the library about a group of intelligent, caring, and involved people who found a glowing stone. They sat watching the thing until they lost the will to use their talent and voices, turning into squabbling monkeys. Only when the one strong person who had refused to look destroyed the thing and began telling stories from the past, did the people return to their former state. Before it's too late, remove the influence of mindless viewing from our schools!

Sincerely,

Robbie Berrier

To the Editor,

I would like to congratulate the local public schools for their venture into a brave new world of education. That is the new world of satellite TV in the classroom. I know there was much controversy over this issue, but good sense and a progressive view prevailed as lobbyists for Hamburger Haven and Sofizz Soda offered to foot the bill for this great educational tool.

Surely everyone knows that the people who would stand in the way of this type of progress are hopelessly mistaken in their concerns over the influence of television. In the schools, the students will be guided and supervised by their teachers who will watch most of the programs right along with their students. At other times, while the students are learning from the television, the teachers can catch up on other paperwork for the class. The programs will all be very educational, and the teachers can give the students a written quiz immediately to make sure that they are retaining the material covered both visually and verbally by the show.

I believe that satellite television is nothing but a good thing for our schools. Where else can you go to experience the thrill of learning found on the TV? The children's parents are happy with the technology and knowing that their children are quietly watching good programs, not running around being resistant to learning. The community is satisfied that the schools are turning out technologically literate students who will fit right in with the rest of our great society. The future, as seen from my point of view, is as bright as my television screen at night.

Sincerely,

Rachel Stein

1. Which writer presents a more convincing argument? Explain 3 – 4 reasons why.

2. Draw a chart like the one on capital punishment. List the main arguments for and against the issue of television in schools.

3. Write a paragraph in which you compare and contrast the arguments on the issue of television in schools. Take a stand on the most convincing position, and provide evidence to support your choice. Use the format of the paragraph 'Stop Capital Punishment' as a model.

C. Find a Local Issue

Read your local newspaper regularly until you find two letters to the editor that argue opposite sides of the same issue. Use these letters as a basis for responding to the questions above from Practice B.

D. Argue Both Sides

Read national magazines and newspapers in hard copy or on a Web site to find a controversial issue that interests you. Write a one paragraph letter to the editor supporting the issue and a one paragraph letter to the editor opposing the issue. If necessary, use resources other than the newspaper or magazine for evidence in support of your arguments. After completing this exercise, talk with your classmates or instructor about how your opinion changed during the process. Exchange your paragraphs with other students or your teacher for feedback. Send your best letter to the local paper for publication.

COMPARING AND CONTRASTING MESSAGES OR THEMES WITHIN AND BETWEEN TEXTS

When analyzing and discussing (or writing) about literature, often you will need to compare and/or contrast the messages or themes in a single piece of literature or in more than one piece of literature. Certainly the first thing to examine is the **theme** or **message** present in each individual piece of literature. If you are discussing a single piece of literature, you need to consider each character and how that character is related to the theme. How do the characters relate to each other? Sometimes, within a single piece of literature, one character may represent or be involved in one particular theme, while another character represents a different theme. By considering these questions, you will then have the points of discussion that will be your basis for comparison and contrast.

If you are comparing more than one piece of literature, there are additional questions to explore. Are the messages the same or are they different in the two reading selections? Which message is more powerfully expressed? Why? What are the similarities and differences in the way the characters in each piece are related to the theme? Answering some or all of the preceding questions should provide you with material for comparison and contrast.

COMPARING AND CONTRASTING CHARACTERS IN FICTION

Writers can develop characters in several different ways, including **description**, **dialogue**, **action**, and **relationships with other characters**. A skilled fiction writer creates interest by developing strong characters with distinct personalities. A simple example is A. A. Milne's children's stories involving Winnie the Pooh. In each story, Pooh is usually optimistic, Piglet anxious, Rabbit self-centered, and Eeyore tragically pessimistic. Regardless of the situation presented, each character acts and reacts in a way that reveals his unique personality.

Sometimes authors use characters to represent or symbolize larger themes. For example, in the *Lord of the Rings* movies, Gandalf the White dresses in white, and through his words and actions, he represents honor, truth, and goodness. On the other hand, the nine Ringwraiths are clothed in black, and they are enslaved to carry out evil purposes — they are the incarnation of evil. The conflict between these characters in the story symbolizes the larger theme of the conflict between good and evil.

A classic example of contrasting characters is found in the story of "The Tortoise and the Hare." Though you are probably familiar with it, read the story carefully, noting similarities and differences between the two main characters.

Comparing and Contrasting

The Tortoise and the Hare

Once upon a time, in a great forest, there lived a hare and a tortoise. Tortoise was slow in everything he did. Sometimes he ate his breakfast so slowly that it was almost lunchtime before he had finished. He kept his house clean and neat, but he did it at his own pace, very slowly.

Hare, on the other hand, was quick as a wink in all that he did. He got up early in the morning, finished his breakfast, and went for a brisk walk in the forest before Tortoise had even gotten out of bed. Hare could not imagine how Tortoise could stand to be so slow all the time.

Hare was sure that he was the smartest, fastest, most handsome animal in the whole forest. And he never failed to tell his friends how splendid he was. "I think I look especially fine today," he would say to himself as he stood in front of his mirror.

Tortoise never bragged about himself. He knew that he was not particularly handsome and that he was very slow, but he did not mind. He was happy to spend his time working hard, painting his beautiful pictures at his very slow pace.

One day Tortoise was sitting beside the stream painting a picture of the pretty wildflowers on its bank. Hare came up and said, "You are such a slowpoke, Tortoise. You've been working on this same picture all week!"

"I'm not so very slow," protested Tortoise.

"Silly fellow," said Hare. "You're so slow that I could beat you at anything you can name. Just name something, and I'll win."

"All right," said Tortoise. "How about a race?"

What an idea! Hare laughed and laughed at the thought of running a race with Tortoise! Hare laughed so hard he thought he would explode.

On the day of the big race, all the animals in the forest gathered to watch. Tortoise and Hare stepped up to the starting line. Tortoise looked nervous when he saw all the animals. Hare smiled and waved to the crowd. He could hardly wait to show Tortoise a thing or two about running a race. Fox looked at both runners. He shouted, "Get ready. Get set. Go!"

The race was on! Hare dashed across the starting line. In a blink of an eye, he disappeared over the first hill. "Oh dear," said Squirrel to herself. "There goes Hare, out of sight already. Poor Tortoise hasn't even started!" Sure enough, Tortoise was just beginning to climb the steep path—very slowly.

Hare ran and ran until he was sure he would win. "This isn't even a race," he said to himself. "I think I'll lie down and rest a bit. Then I'll finish and still have plenty of time to spare. There's no way that slowpoke will ever catch up with me!" So Hare lay down under a shady tree and soon fell fast asleep.

Suddenly, Hare awoke with a start. He could hear cheering. He jumped up and started running as fast as his long legs would carry him. But when he saw the finish line of the race, he could not believe his eyes. Tortoise was about to win the race. Hare could not believe it. Tortoise was crossing the finish line!

The crowd cheered and cheered. They ran to the finish line to congratulate Tortoise. The wise Owl blinked his eyes and said what all the other animals were thinking, "Slow and steady wins the race!"

To compare the two characters, you may develop an H-map similar to the one below.

Differences Tortoise	Similarities	Differences Hare
• slow • humble • works hard • walks steadily • never gives up on race • wins race	• they are animals • they live in a forest • they have other animal friends • they run in race	• fast • boastful • works little • runs quickly • sleeps during race • loses race

In the story of "The Tortoise and the Hare," the author contrasts the two main characters, so the differences and similarities between them are relatively simple. On the MCA Grade 8 Reading Test, you may find more complex stories and characters. In this case, consider the aspects of character, listed below, to help you make your comparisons and contrasts.

Character Aspects		
gender	family situation	personality traits
age	physical appearance	thoughts and feelings
occupation	style of dress	role in the story (protagonist, etc.)
goals	way of speaking	relationship to other characters

Practice 3: Comparing and Contrasting Characters

A. The Tortoise and the Hare

Based on the H-map of the tortoise and the hare, write a one paragraph response to the following question: Which character appeals to you the most—the tortoise or the hare? Include 3 – 4 reasons for your response.

B. Character Experiment

Read Nathaniel Hawthorne's short story "Dr. Heidegger's Experiment." The characters all face a similar experience but react to it in different ways. Choose two characters, develop an H-map, and write a paragraph comparing and contrasting them. Share your paragraph in a small group with other students or with your teacher.

C. Other Stories

Review a novel or short story that you have read recently, and create an H-map comparing and contrasting two of the characters from the story. Possible choices may include Mark Twain's *Adventures of Huckleberry Finn*, John Steinbeck's *The Pearl* or *Of Mice and Men*, S. E. Hinton's *The Outsiders*, Harper Lee's *To Kill a Mockingbird*, Edgar Allan Poe's "The Cask of Amontillado," or Bret Harte's "The Outcasts of Poker Flat."

D. Business Card Design

Design a business card for two or more characters based on stories you have read. Each card should reflect the unique personality of each character. Ask for feedback on your cards from other students or from your instructor. See the sample business card below.

Sample business card for the Tin Man from *The Wizard of Oz*.

CHAPTER 10 SUMMARY

Comparing and **contrasting** is the process of looking for similarities and differences between two or more objects, characters, or ideas. One of the most important aspects of comparing and contrasting is to look for similarities or differences **within the same category**. There are several areas of written materials that can be compared and contrasted:

• **Reading Passages**	The following two strategies can help when looking for comparison and contrast within a reading passage.
	• Look for **signal words** which indicate similarities and differences.
	• Create an **H-map** which categorizes differences between each item that is being compared.
• **Arguments**	Often, you may need to compare and contrast opposing arguments. In order to do that, you need to look at some other aspects of the argument first.
	• **Analyze the support** for each argument.
	• **Evaluate the validity** of each position.
	• Then **compare and contrast** opposing arguments.
• **Characters**	There are many aspects of characters that can be compared and contrasted. Writers can develop characters in several different ways, including **description, dialogue, action**, and **relationships with other characters**. In order to compare and contrast characters, you will want to look at the ways they have been developed, and then compare and contrast the various areas.
• **Messages or Themes**	Comparing and contrasting messages or themes involves an analysis of the details that support them.

CHAPTER 10 REVIEW

Read the following scene from a 1906 story by O. Henry. Then read "Dating in Different Countries." Answer the questions that follow both selections.

Excerpt from "The Coming-Out of Maggie"

This scene from the story takes place at a private dance held by the "Give and Take" Athletic Association. Two young men are about to fight over Maggie.

Some fine instinct that Rome must have bequeathed to us caused nearly every one to turn and look at them—there was a subtle feeling that two gladiators had met in the arena. Two or three Give and Takes with tight coat sleeves drew nearer.

"One moment, Mr. O'Sullivan," said Dempsey. "I hope you're enjoying yourself. Where did you say you lived?"

The two gladiators were well matched. Dempsey had, perhaps, ten pounds of weight to give away. The O'Sullivan had breadth with quickness. Dempsey had a glacial eye, a dominating slit of a mouth, an indestructible jaw, a complexion like a belle's, and the coolness of a champion. The visitor showed more fire in his contempt and less control over his conspicuous sneer. They were enemies by the law written when the rocks were molten. They were each too splendid, too mighty, too incomparable to divide preeminence. One only must survive.

"I live on Grand," said O'Sullivan, insolently; "and no trouble to find me at home. Where do you live?" Dempsey ignored the question.

"You say your name's O'Sullivan," he went on. "Well, 'Big Mike' says he never saw you before."

"Lots of things he never saw," said the favourite of the hop.

"As a rule," went on Dempsey, huskily sweet, "O'Sullivans in this district know one another. You escorted one of our lady members here, and we want a chance to make good. If you've got a family tree let's see a few historical O'Sullivan buds come out on it. Or do you want us to dig it out of you by the roots?"

Read the following interview. Then, write constructed responses for the questions that follow.

Dating in Different Countries

American teenage girls must find their own husbands, and no one else can do it for them.

This concept is very difficult for teenagers in India to understand as you can tell from the following interview with two Indian teenage girls.

"Don't you want to be able to choose your own husbands?" I asked.

"No! Never!" the girls answered vehemently. Nisha, a very beautiful girl with wide, almond-shaped eyes went on to say "I don't want to worry about whether I'll get married or not. I know I'll get married. I know my parents are a better judge of character than I am. I am too young to make such a decision. When my parents choose someone for me, I know it will be someone that will be able to support me and someone that my family already likes and respects."

"What if I lived in America and I chose a boy my family didn't like? Before it was over, everyone might be against me. There might be bad feelings at home with my parents because of my choice, and if I argued with my husband, who would support me?"

It was Rasheed's turn. "It seems the American system would be very humiliating for me. I would have to spend a lot more time making myself beautiful and attractive and try to figure out ways to get boys to notice me. And if the boy I liked didn't notice me, maybe I would feel like a failure as a person. I would have to compete with other girls to be the prettiest—it seems so demeaning and stressful. And what if I were shy? Would I get married?"

"Possibly not," I answered honestly.

Nisha asked the hardest question, "In America, does the girl get to choose? Isn't it the boy who chooses anyway?" A good question.

1. Compare and contrast how women and men choose a husband or wife for marriage in the United States and in India, based on the "Coming-Out of Maggie" story and the "Dating in Different Countries" article.

2. What are the strengths and weaknesses of each approach to finding a marriage partner?

3. Which do you think is the better way to choose a marriage partner? Why?

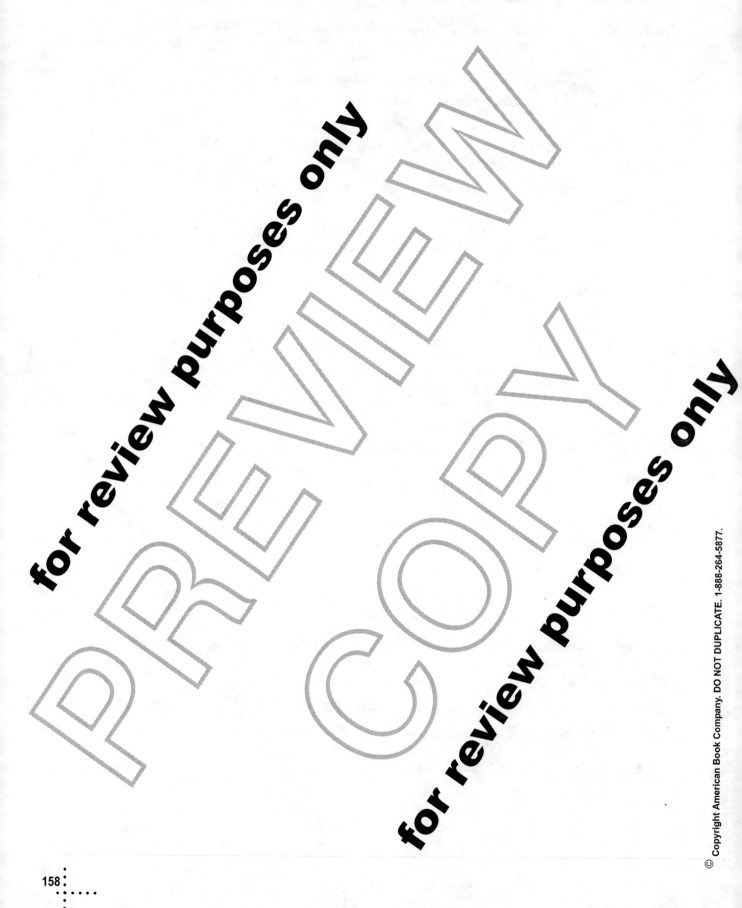

MCA-II Reading Grade 8
Practice Test 1

The purpose of this practice test is to measure your progress in reading comprehension and critical thinking. This practice test is based on the Minnesota standards for English and Language Arts and adheres to the sample question format provided by the Minnesota Department of Education.

General Directions:

1. Read all directions carefully.

2. Read each question or sample. Then choose the best answer.

3. Choose only one answer for each question. If you change an answer, be sure to erase your original answer completely.

4. You are allowed to take notes in the test book.

Practice Test 1

Segment 1

> Read about Mahalia Jackson, a famous gospel singer. Then answer questions 1 – 9. Some questions may ask you about certain paragraphs. The paragraph numbers are found along the left side of the passage.

Goin' Up to the High Places: Mahalia Jackson Remembered

1   Mahalia Jackson was the greatest gospel singer of her time. She was born one of six children on October 26, 1911. Mahalia's family lived in a shack by the river on Water Street in New Orleans. She achieved greatness in spite of being born into poverty and disadvantage.

2   Mahalia Jackson soon began doing what was natural for her—singing. At a young age, she began singing in the choir at her father's church. Tragedy struck the family when her mother died. Mahalia was only five years old. Her father sent Mahalia and her brother to live with an aunt. She was an abusive woman who beat them frequently.

3   Jackson worked hard during her childhood to help support her family. As a young girl, she held jobs as a maid and a laundress. Jackson recalled, "When the old people weren't home, I'd turn on a Bessie Smith record to make the work go faster." Even though Jackson never performed jazz, Bessie Smith influenced her more than anyone else.

4   When Jackson was sixteen, she moved to Chicago to pursue her ambition of becoming a nurse. She worked as a domestic once again and sang at the South Side Greater Baptist Church. She gained a large following within the black community because of her beautiful and powerful voice.

5   While in Chicago, she met the man she would marry, Isaac Hockenhull. He encouraged her to start her own business. Mahalia first opened a beauty shop and later a flower shop. Her flower shop was successful, but her clients insisted Mahalia sing at their ceremonies too. Isaac encouraged her to take voice lessons. He believed she might be more suited to a career in the music industry.

6   Thomas A. Dorsey, considered the Father of Gospel Music, soon discovered Jackson's talent. He promoted her around the country at church programs and conventions. Jackson's husband and others encouraged her to leave gospel music behind and pursue jazz and blues recordings. They felt the change to jazz and blues would appeal to the mainstream of society. Jackson would not change.

7   She continued singing with her powerful gospel edge and recorded several hits. Her first hit, "Move on up a Little Higher," sold more than a million copies. Although her popularity was rooted in the black community, white audiences also came to appreciate her music. By 1954, her song, "Didn't It Rain," made the Hit Parade.

8   Jackson went on to sing across the United States and Europe. In Great Britain, she sang for Queen Elizabeth. In New York City, she performed four sold-out concerts at Carnegie Hall. She also sang a song prior to Martin Luther King Jr.'s famous "I Have a Dream" speech in 1963.

9   Before Jackson's death in 1972, she had sung her gospel music across four continents. People will always remember for her stirring voice. "I sing God's music because it makes me feel free. It gives me hope," she said. Mahalia received a final honor posthumously. The Rock and Roll Hall of Fame inducted Mahalia Jackson twenty five years after her death.

1. What sentence from the passage is an opinion?   I.C.1

    A. As a young girl, she held jobs as a maid and a laundress.

    B. Mahalia first opened a beauty shop and later a flower shop.

    C. Mahalia Jackson was the greatest gospel singer of her time.

    D. Jackson went on to sing across the United States and Europe.

2. What type of music did Bessie Smith perform?   I.C.4

    A. pop   **C.** rock

    B. jazz   **D.** gospel

3. As it is used in paragraph 6, the word promoted means   I.B.3

    A. raised in rank.

    B. booked for events.

    C. contributed to prosperity.

    D. advanced to a higher grade.

4. Read the following sentence from paragraph 7 of the passage.   I.C.14

> By 1954, her song, "Didn't it Rain," made the Hit Parade

The author included this information to show

    A. Mahalia's popularity was growing.

    B. Mahalia made more than one record.

    C. why Mahalia sold her flower shop.

    D. Isaac's support for Mahalia's music.

5. Which sentence shows why Mahalia Jackson chose to sing gospel music?   I.C.1

    A. When the old people weren't home, I'd turn on a Bessie Smith record to make the work go faster.

    B. Her flower shop was successful, but her clients insisted Mahalia sing at their ceremonies too.

    C. In Great Britain, she sang for Queen Elizabeth.

    D. I sing God's music because it makes me feel free.

6. In paragraph 9 of the passage, the word posthumously means   I.B.2

    A. with approval.

    B. with gratitude.

    C. after dying.

    D. after singing.

7. The author wrote this passage most likely to   I.C.14

    A. persuade readers to pursue a music career.

    B. compare careers in jazz and gospel music.

    C. explain how a person trains to become a gospel singer.

    D. describe the life and accomplishments of Mahalia Jackson.

8. Which is the best summary of the passage?   I.C.1

    A. Mahalia Jackson received support and encouragement from her husband, family, and friends.

    B. Despite difficulties in life, Mahalia Jackson stayed true to herself and forged a successful career in gospel music.

    C. Mahalia Jackson performed many different jobs during her lifetime.

    D. Gospel music is enjoyed and appreciated by people around the world.

Please write the answer to question 9 in your answer book.

9. One theme found in this passage was hope. Give four examples from the passage when Mahalia Jackson needed hope to persevere.

I.D.12

Some people see a rundown, abandoned house as haunted. Read the following poem to learn how the author feels about such a place. Then answer questions 10–16. To help you answer some of the questions, some lines of the poem are numbered.

The House with Nobody in it

Joyce Kilmer

1   Whenever I walk to Suffern along the Erie track
    I go by a poor old farmhouse with its shingles broken and black.
    I suppose I've passed it a hundred times, but I always stop for a minute
    And look at the house, the tragic house, the house with nobody in it.

5   I never have seen a haunted house, but I hear there are such things;
    That they hold the talk of spirits, their mirth and sorrowings.
    I know this house isn't haunted, and I wish it were, I do;
    For it wouldn't be so lonely if it had a ghost or two.

9   This house on the road to Suffern needs a dozen panes of glass,
    And somebody ought to weed the walk and take a scythe to the grass.
    It needs new paint and shingles, and the vines should be trimmed and tied;
    But what it needs the most of all is some people living inside.

13 If I had a lot of money and all my debts were paid
    I'd put a gang of men to work with brush and saw and spade.
    I'd buy that place and fix it up the way it used to be
    And I'd find some people who wanted a home and give it to them free.

17 Now, a new house standing empty, with staring window and door,
    Looks idle, perhaps, and foolish, like a hat on its block in the store.
    But there's nothing mournful about it, it cannot be sad and lone
    For the lack of something within it that it has never known.

21 But a house that has done what a house should do, a house that has sheltered life,
    That has put its loving wooden arms around a man and his wife,
    A house that has echoed a baby's laugh and held up his stumbling feet,
    Is the saddest sight, when it's left alone, that ever your eyes could meet

25 So whenever I go to Suffern along the Erie track
    I never go by the empty house without stopping and looking back,
    Yet it hurts me to look at the crumbling roof and the shutters fallen apart,
28 For I can't help thinking the poor old house is a house with a broken heart.

10. The author uses personification in the fifth stanza to help the reader   I.D.7

   A. hear the house.

   B. visualize the house.

   C. sympathize with the house.

   D. understand the history of the house.

11. Read the dictionary entry below   I.B.2

> **tragic**—(1) unpleasant; (2) disastrous; (3) marked by sorrow; (4) wretched mistake

Which is the meaning of the word tragic in line 4 of the poem?

   A. unpleasant

   B. disastrous

   C. wretched mistake

   D. marked by sorrow

12. The reader can conclude that the author most likely believes   I.C.4

   A. people should not buy new houses.

   B. every house should have a family.

   C. all abandoned houses are haunted.

   D. every family should have a house.

13. What is the main idea of the fourth stanza?   I.C.1

   A. The house should be returned to its original appearance.

   B. The author wants to repair the house and give it a family.

   C. The author wishes he had more money and fewer debts.

   D. Many people would be needed to repair the house and yard.

14. Read the following lines from the poem.   I.D.7

> Now, a new house standing empty, with staring window and door,
> Looks idle, perhaps, and foolish, like a hat on its block in the store.

The phrase, like a hat on its block, is an example of

   A. metaphor.

   B. simile.

   C. onomatopoeia.

   D. personification.

15. Which of the following statements best reflects the theme of this poem?   I.C.14

   A. Houses must be repaired, or they fall apart.

   B. The inside of a house is more important than the outside.

   C. Some people like old houses.

   D. A house is not a home without a family in it.

16. Which is the best summary of this poem?   I.C.1

   A. The author feels sad when he passes an old, abandoned house. She wants to repair it and give it what it really needs — a family.

   B. Older abandoned houses require a great deal of work and money to make them livable again.

   C. It would be better to give away older homes than to leave them empty.

   D. Although some empty farmhouses may be haunted, others are not.

Segment 2

Success in school requires planning and organization. Read this passage. Then answer questions 17 – 25. Some questions require you to reread certain paragraphs.

You Can Succeed

1 The road to academic success is paved with positive learning characteristics. According to the experts — successful people — choosing to adopt those characteristics means choosing to succeed. You will need a positive attitude to carry you over the bumps in the road. No matter how long or difficult the path may seem, always remind yourself — you can succeed.

2 First, set goals for yourself. Setting goals is a trait shared by top executives and honor students. In response to a national survey on reaching success, an executive replied, "If you don't know where you are headed, you will never get there." When setting your goals, reach for the stars, but keep your feet firmly planted on the earth. Unrealistic goals lead to frustration. Realistic goals lead to success. You can succeed.

3 Second, design a plan to help you achieve your goal and commit your plan to paper. Schedule study hours into your day. A government study on academic success revealed that students who had a study schedule were five times more likely to study than students without a schedule. If you are concerned you might have trouble adhering to the schedule, then make a sign in sheet for yourself. Hang it in an obvious place where you can't avoid looking. Once you have committed your time, find the perfect location for studying. Choose a quiet place without distractions. If you can escape the television or your little sister practicing the drums at home, go out. Quiet spaces are frequently available in libraries and community centers. Setting your plan in motion might not be easy, but you can do it. You can succeed.

4 Next, go to school prepared to learn. After a full night of sleep, eat a nutritious breakfast. It is more difficult to succeed with an empty stomach. Write a checklist of the supplies you need to bring to school. Double-check your list to be sure you haven't overlooked anything. Sometimes it is the simple little things that can interfere with your success. Before you leave for school, remind yourself of your goals. Always remember, you can succeed.

5 Your next step on the road to success is making the most of your class time. Be certain to bring the tools you need to succeed with you to class. Your textbook should be handy and your notebook should be organized, so you don't need to shuffle through papers to find important information. Practice good listening skills in class. Focus on the speaker. A good listener isn't looking at the clock, doodling in the margins of a notebook, or thinking about what film to see the next weekend. Pour your whole self into the listening process, and you will remember more of what was said. Another good way to increase your understanding and recall of the subject is to participate in class discussions. Raise your hand. Ask questions. Volunteer answers. Be an active learner, not a passive member of the audience. Remember, you can succeed.

6   Finally, pause at regular intervals to evaluate your progress. What parts of your plan are working? What parts need some adjusting? Stay with what is working and revise whatever isn't working for you. Many survey participants reported experiencing failure before success. They noted that perseverance was the key to their achievements. One participant expressed that viewpoint when he wrote, "As they say, try, try, again. I know that's why I'm where I am today." The road to success may be a long and bumpy path, but you can make it. You can succeed.

17. In paragraph 2, when the speaker says, "When setting your goals, reach for the stars, but keep you feet firmly planted on the earth," what does the speaker mean?   I.D.4

   A.   Set high but achievable goals.

   B.   Success makes you feel taller.

   C.   The answers you need are in the stars.

   D.   Learn all you can about the universe.

18. Which sources did the author use to support her position?   I.C.6

   A.   interviews with executives and students

   B.   personal observations in schools and offices

   C.   a government study and a national survey

   D.   personal experience and a study skills book

19. What is the main idea of paragraph 3?   I.C.1

   A.   The perfect study spot is free of distractions.

   B.   It is difficult to study in a noisy environment.

   C.   The government is interested in learning how students succeed.

   D.   It is important to design and commit to a plan to reach your goals.

20. The author wrote this article most likely to   I.C.14

   A.   explain study skills.

   B.   motivate students for success.

   C.   compare work habits of students and executives.

   D.   describe the benefits of hard work and success.

21. Why does the author recommend students participate in class discussions?   I.C.4

   A.   to increase understanding and recall of the subject

   B.   to command the attention of the teacher and class

   C.   to remind yourself of your plans and goals

   D.   to avoid forgetting textbooks and notebooks

22. Which detail sentence would best support paragraph 4?   I.C.1

   A.   School supplies often cost less during the summer.

   B.   Some people enjoy fruit and yogurt for breakfast.

   C.   There are many opportunities to volunteer your services to your school.

   D.   Several studies show a direct connection between sleep and productivity.

23. What is the meaning of the word perseverance found in paragraph 6?   I.B.3

   A.   the art of active listening

   B.   the process of setting goals

   C.   the ability to go on despite discouragement

   D.   the method of dividing a task into small steps

24. The author would most likely agree with which statement?   I.C.14

    A. There is power in positive thinking.
    B. The higher you reach the greater the challenge.
    C. Where you go to school determines where you go in life.
    D. Success will be easy to achieve if you don't worry about the detail.

Please write the answer to question 25 in your answer book.

25. Summarize the steps the author recommends to achieve success.   I.C.

Segment 3

What would you do if you went camping without your tent poles? Read the following story to see how two campers solved their problem. Then answer questions 20 – 34.

Some questions will require you to review the numbered paragraphs.

Wings and Strings

1   Fran and her college roommate, Philena, enjoyed listening to bluegrass music. Fran's father was in a band, so she grew up listening to the lively music. It didn't take long for Philena to get hooked on it too. Soon, the sounds of guitars and fiddles could be heard coming from their dorm room every night.

2   One fall, Fran's parents invited the girls to join them at the Wings and Strings Festival. Every year, the bluegrass festival was held on the grounds of an old airfield surrounded by vintage airplanes. Fran's parents never missed the festival. Each year, they met friends, family, and fellow musicians there. Fran had not joined them since she entered college.

3   Fran and Philena jumped at a chance to get away from school for a weekend. The festival was being held in Rochester, so the girls would go directly from school and meet Fran's parents at the festival. Fran called her parents and accepted the invitation. She told them she was going to pass on their offer of a hotel room. Instead, the roommates would camp on the festival grounds.

4   While Philena was in class on Friday, Fran packed Philena's truck. As soon as Philena's class ended, the girls left Moorhead for Rochester. Four hours later, they arrived at the airfield where the festival was taking place. Fran and Philena immediately began setting up the tent. They unloaded their gear from the back of the truck and made an unpleasant discovery. Fran had packed the tent but left the tent poles behind. Fran thought about her parents in their comfortable hotel room. She looked at Philena, who was studying the empty space in the back of the truck. Fran joined her friend when she saw a smile spread across Philena's face. Philena had an idea. The air mattress would fit in the back of the truck. Not only was the truck big enough, but the truck cap would keep out the chilly, October night air.

5   With the tent crisis averted, the girls began searching through their gear for the air mattress pump. As soon as they located the pump, they went to work on the mattress. It didn't take them long to discover the poorly repaired hole in the air pump. After one compression, the adhesive gave away on the duct tape and a gust of air blew back in Philena's face. Fran groaned and sat down on the ground, covering her head with her arms. However, Philena was not about to concede defeat. After all, they were independent college students accustomed to solving problems by thinking outside of the box. She was certain they could solve this problem without having to seek help or shelter from Fran's parents. Philena fiddled with the pump for a few minutes, and then the girls got back to work. Philena wasn't able to completely seal the hole, so the work went very slowly. Finally, two hours and several hand cramps later, the girls had filled the air mattress to their liking.

6   As they slid the mattress into the back of the truck, a man, who was sitting nearby in a camp chair, yelled out to them. He told the girls he had an electric pump that would have filled the mattress in about in ten minutes. He chuckled and said he would have offered it to them, but they looked set on doing it their own way. He said he admired that kind of independence in young people. The girls smiled politely and groaned in frustration. They had missed most of the day's activities.

7   Finally free from their preparations, the roommates headed toward the stage to find Fran's parents and friends. Fran's father asked Philena to dance and taught her the Louisiana two-step. By midnight, the girls were danced out and tired. They headed back to the truck and a hard-earned night's rest on their old adversary, the air mattress.

26. The name of the festival, Wings and Strings, refers to   I.C.4

A.   independence and family ties.

B.   the name of Fran's father's band.

C.   the best solution to the girls' problem.

D.   airplane wings and instrument strings.

27. What is the main idea of paragraph 3?   I.C.1

A.   Fran and Philena wanted to go camping.

B.   The festival was being held on a weekend.

C.   Fran and Philena planned to attend the festival.

D.   Fran's parents planned to stay in a hotel room.

28. Which is the correct meaning of pass as it is used in paragraph 3?   I.B.3

A.   to move ahead

B.   to become approved

C.   to not accept something

D.   to go across, over, or through

29. Which choice best describes Fran?   I.D.3

A.   disorganized

B.   responsible

C.   studious

D.   flexible

30. Which sentence from the story best shows Philena's determination?   I.D.3

A.   However, Philena was not about to concede defeat.

B.   It didn't take long for Philena to get hooked on it too.

C.   Fran's father asked Philena to dance and taught her the Louisiana two-step.

D.   As soon as they located the pump, they went to work on the mattress.

31. Why didn't the girls sleep in the tent?   I.C.4

A.   The air was too chilly to sleep out in the tent.

B.   They couldn't put up the tent without the poles.

C.   Fran's parents insisted they stay with them at the hotel.

D.   Blowing up the mattress was faster than setting up the tent.

32. In paragraph 4, why was Philena studying the back of the truck?   I.C.4

A.   She was looking for the tent poles.

B.   She was looking for the air pump.

C.   She was getting ready to pack her gear in the truck and return to school.

D.   She was checking to be sure there was enough space for the air mattress.

33. As it is used in paragraph 5, <u>fiddled</u> means   I.B.3

A. moved restlessly.

B. cheated or swindled.

C. made minor adjustments.

D. played a musical instrument.

34. How most likely would Fran have solved this problem on her own?   I.C.4

A. She would have fixed the pump herself.

B. She would have slept outside under the stars.

C. She would have joined her parents at the hotel.

D. She would have borrowed the pump from the man.

Thailand is famous for exotic dishes and healthy food choices. Read about why Thai food is good for you, then answer questions 35 – 41. Some questions may ask you about certain paragraphs. The paragraphs are numbered on the left side of the passage. Refer to the numbered paragraphs on the left side of the article when necessary.

A Healthy Choice

1   In recent years, Thai restaurants have gained in popularity. The restaurants especially appeal to health conscience diners. Thai food is absolutely the healthiest food you can eat. It contains much less fat than typical Western food and numerous herbs and spices that improve digestion. Block Medical Center recently concluded a study on patients with high cholesterol levels. Patients substituted lower fat foods five times a week for their typical meals. The majority of the patients lowered their cholesterol by twenty percent or more.

2   Contributing to the healthy nature of the food are the methods used to prepare it. Thai foods are often grilled, boiled, or stewed. These methods lower fat and help maintain the nutritional value of the food. Western foods are often pan fried or deep fried. Those methods add unwanted fat and calories to the diet.

3   Salad is often a favored option for people watching their waistline and is available in both Thai and Western restaurants. Thai salad is a mix of greens, meat or seafood, and sauce. The sauce is a blend of a tempting variety of herbs in a shrimp or curry paste. The salad has scarcely any fat even with the savory sauce. Western salads also include greens and meat or seafood. Unlike Thai salads, Western restaurants always serve salads swimming in a pool of bland, high fat mayonnaise based dressings. The salads come in portions more suited to a party than an individual. The healthier choice is obvious

4   Desserts are also available at both Thai and Western restaurants. Everyone loves the pumpkin custard at a Thai restaurant. A banana cooked in coconut milk is another popular choice. Clearly, when you dine in a Thai restaurant, even dessert can be good for you. Western desserts tend to be heavier and full of fat and refined sugar. Chocolate cake, iced brownies, and hot fudge sundaes often contain more fat and calories than the meal itself. No responsible person would choose the Western desserts.

5   Healthy eaters will tell you to "follow your nose" when choosing a restaurant. Thai food has a distinct, mouth watering aroma. The pungent scent of lemon grass, ginger-like galangal, garlic, basil, and kaffir lime fills the restaurant and pours out the door. Not only do these ingredients smell good and taste delicious, they are also good for you! Many people believe these items can cure a headache, relieve arthritis pain, and even cure the common cold. No greasy cheeseburger can do all that.

6   In addition to strengthening your body, dining in a Thai restaurant strengthens your family spirit. Unlike Western restaurants where waiters serve each diner as a lone visitor, Thai restaurants serve meals family style. There is never a time when you are waiting for your dinner companion's meal to come out of the kitchen while your meal sits on the table growing cold.

7   As everyone can clearly see, Thai food really is the healthiest food you can eat. No other food comes close to providing a balanced, nutritional diet. Sweet or sour, spicy or mild, Thai food has something for everyone. And as one diner at the Thai restaurant in my neighborhood noted, "No other food tastes as good!"

35. Which of the following statements best reflects the theme of this passage?   I.C.14

   A.   You are what you eat.
   B.   Think before you act.
   C.   Variety is the spice of life.
   D.   Beauty is as beauty does.

36. Which sentence should be added to paragraph 1 to strengthen the author's argument?   I.C.1

   A.   Block Medical Center conducts many different nutritional studies.
   B.   The lower fat foods used in the study came from a Thai restaurant.
   C.   Western restaurants outnumber Thai restaurants twenty to one in America.
   D.   My cousin and her family love Thai food and eat it every night for dinner.

37. Which sentence from the passage is a fact?   I.C.11

   A.   Thai food is absolutely the healthiest food you can eat.
   B.   Everyone loves the pumpkin custard at a Thai restaurant.
   C.   No responsible person would choose the Western desserts.
   D.   Desserts are also available at both Thai and Western restaurants.

38. How are Thai and Western salads alike?   I.D.12

   A.   They both have a low-fat savory sauce.
   B.   They both come in over-sized portions.
   C.   They both contain greens and meat or seafood.
   D.   They both arrive swimming in a heavy dressing.

39. What is the main idea of paragraph 4?   I.C.1

   A.   No meal is complete without dessert.
   B.   No one should eat chocolate desserts.
   C.   You can enjoy a healthy dessert in a Thai restaurant.
   D.   People prefer lighter desserts over rich, heavy desserts.

40. Which is an example of dessert in a Thai restaurant?   I.C.1

   A.   pumpkin custard
   B.   iced brownies
   C.   chocolate cake
   D.   hot fudge sundaes

41. The author uses several techniques that show her bias in the article.   I.D.12   I.C.6

   A.   List two ways the author's bias shows in the article.
   B.   Use examples from the article to support your answer.

Segment 4

Today most people own clocks and watches. However, timekeeping was not always easy or exact. Read the following article about the history of clock making. Then answer questions 42 – 48. For some answers, review numbered paragraphs as needed.

What Time Is It?

1 People have always wanted to track time. Thousands of years ago, early man noticed that shadows cast by trees and mountains pointed in different directions at various times of the day. They used this observation to design a sundial. Sundials were used for centuries by many different civilizations.

2 The sundial was limited by nature. It was impossible to tell time at night or on a stormy day. Early civilizations found ways to track time that were not dependent on the availability of sunlight. One example is the Egyptian water clock or clepsydra. This device measured time through the use of water and a float. The clock had two chambers. As water escaped from one chamber, the float rose in the other chamber.

3 The appearance of clocks as we know them today began in China. The Chinese fabricated a device called an escapement. The escapement is still an integral part of clock-making today. It is a small break that stops the wheels of the clock regularly, preventing the power source from running unchecked. This stop and go movement is what makes a clock tick.

4 A major breakthrough in clock making came in 1500. Peter Henlein developed something he called, "spring power." Spring power helped clock makers build clocks that ran more accurately and took up less space. With spring power, clocks could fit on a table or mantle. More than a century later, a Dutch scientist, Christian Huygens, built on this idea. He developed a spring assembly that is similar to what we use in wrist watches today.

5 Around 1660, London clockmakers invented the tall case clock. Known as grandfather clocks, these were first made for royalty, nobility, and churches. The clocks were wide and tall to allow for the swing of the long pendulum.

6 At about the same time, wooden clock works were developed in Germany and Switzerland. Whereas metal was expensive and difficult to work with, wood was plentiful and craftsmen were skilled in woodworking. Wooden clocks were reliable, and the parts rarely needed lubrication. With the use of wooden parts, clocks started appearing in more and more households.

7 The Industrial Revolution decreased the cost of metal and increased the technology needed for metal working. The production of metal clocks became faster and cheaper than the production of wooden clocks. Wooden gears were hard to make with the new machinery available and resulted in a large amount of wood being scrapped. As a result, wooden clocks continued to be made by hand.

8   The speeding up of human activity has been the reason for the progress made in timekeeping. Clock making has evolved to include precision timekeeping instruments we need today. Whether we measure time by the sun, a ticking clock, or a digital watch, one thing is true for all of us. How we use our time is more important than how we measure it.

42. Why was the sundial limited by nature?   I.C.4

    A. The year has four seasons.

    B. It depended on sunlight.

    C. Metal ores were hard to find.

    D. It required a flat, level surface.

43. Who most likely is the intended audience for this article?   I.C.

    A. a student trying to purchase a new watch

    B. a student planning a European vacation

    C. a student interested in the history of clock making

    D. a student looking for a part-time job selling watches

44. Why were early grandfather clocks owned only by royalty, nobility, and churches?   I.C.4

    A. They were too expensive for average households.

    B. Average households preferred Swiss clock design.

    C. Only royalty, nobility, and the clergy could read clocks.

    D. The clocks were too tall and too loud for most houses.

45. As a result of the Industrial Revolution, clocks with wooden parts were   I.C.4

    A. made by machines.

    B. made only in London.

    C. less common than clocks with metal parts.

    D. produced faster than before the revolution.

46. The author's use of chronological order in the article gives the reader a sense of   I.D.12

    A. time moving forward.

    B. clock design worldwide.

    C. the excitement of clock making.

    D. the need for changing technology.

47. Which of the following statements best reflects the theme for the article?   I.C.14

    A. Clever is as clever does.

    B. Time stops for no man.

    C. Time flies when you are having fun.

    D. Necessity is the mother of invention.

48. Which is the best summary of the article?   I.C.1

    A. London clockmakers preferred to use metal clock parts, while Swiss and German clockmakers preferred to use wooden clock parts.

    B. The Industrial Revolution changed clock making methods and increased the popularity of metal clock parts.

    C. There are many ways of tracking time. Some popular early methods used things found in nature like the sun and water.

    D. People have tracked time throughout history. Inventors built on the knowledge of earlier generations to design more exact time keeping methods.

MCA-II Reading Grade 8
Practice Test 2

The purpose of this practice test is to measure your progress in reading comprehension and critical thinking. This practice test is based on the Minnesota standards for English and Language Arts and adheres to the sample question format provided by the Minnesota Department of Education.

General Directions:

1. Read all directions carefully.

2. Read each question or sample. Then choose the best answer.

3. Choose only one answer for each question. If you change an answer, be sure to erase your original answer completely.

4. You are allowed to take notes in the test book.

Segment 1

Everyone loves popcorn. Read about the history of popcorn. Then answer questions 1 – 8. Reread the paragraphs to answer the questions. Some questions refer to certain paragraphs. The paragraphs are numbered on the left side of the passage.

A Popping Good Time

An old legend says that one particular summer it got so hot the corn in the fields started popping right off the stalks. The cows and pigs thought it was a snow blizzard, and they lay down and froze to death.

1   Today, we think of popcorn as a light snack, but popcorn has an interesting history. Some people prefer snacking on salty pretzels and fresh fruit. Did you know that ancient Mexicans popped corn more than 80,000 years ago? The Aztec Indians used the popped corn in many ceremonies. Young Aztec women danced wearing popcorn garlands. Popcorn served as decoration for ceremonial headdresses and necklaces too. The Aztecs also used popcorn to decorate statues of the gods. For example, strung kernels adorned the statue of Tlaloc, the <u>deity</u> of maize.

2   Europeans learned about popcorn, one of many varieties of maize, from Amerindians. When Cortes, a Spanish explorer, invaded Mexico in 1519 and Columbus arrived in the West Indies, each saw natives eating popcorn and using it in ceremonies. Maize made up eighty percent of the Amerindian diet. It was an especially versatile food. It could be roasted over the fire, heated and dried, or could be ground into flour with stones. A common way to prepare popcorn at that time was to hold an oiled ear on a stick over a fire. Then the people chewed the exploded kernels right off the ear.

3   Native Americans brought popcorn to the first Thanksgiving. However, it wasn't until the 19th century that popping corn became a popular activity in the U.S. Now, every American loves eating freshly popped popcorn. The first popcorn companies in the United States appeared in the late 1860s. At the same time, popcorn recipes appeared in cookbooks. By the 1890s, vendors sold popcorn at special events. The distinctive smell of hot buttered popcorn wafted through stadiums, circuses, and parks.

5   Peanuts and popcorn launched the snack food industry. In 1896, brothers Fred and Louis Ruekheim came up with the idea of combining popcorn and peanuts. They covered the mixture with sweet, sticky molasses. Called "Cracker Jack," it later had surprise toys inserted directly into every package.

5   The Great Depression and the advent of film with sound brought popcorn and movie theaters together. During the Depression, popcorn was five or ten cents a bag. It was one of the few luxuries down-and-out families could afford. While other businesses failed, the popcorn business thrived.

6   When television became popular in the 1950s, people attended fewer movies. Popcorn sales went down temporarily. However, a new relationship developed between television and popcorn, and sales rebounded.

7   The next big boom in popcorn business from the invention of microwave popcorn. Popcorn went from cold kernels to hot fluffy popcorn in minutes without dirtying a pan. Microwave popcorn accounted for about $240 million in annual sales over the last decade.

8   Americans today consume billion quarts of popcorn each year. The average American eats about 58 quarts. There's a good chance that people reading this page have eaten their fair share of the little white puffballs. What the next phase will be for the versatile kernels, no one knows. What seems certain is that popcorn will endure as a simple and delicious snack with a colorful past.

1. Which detail sentence does not support the main idea in paragraph 1?   I.C.1

   A.   Some people prefer snacking on salty pretzels and fresh fruit.

   B.   The Aztecs also used popcorn to decorate statues of the gods.

   C.   The Aztec Indians used the popped corn in many ceremonies.

   D.   Young Aztec women would dance wearing popcorn garlands.

2. Where did the Aztec Indians live?   I.C.4

   A.   Mexico   C.   United States

   B.   Spain   D.   West Indies

3. In paragraph 1, the word deity means   I.B.2

   A.   man.   C.   popcorn.

   B.   god.   D.   ornament.

4. How did Amerindians eat popcorn?   I.C.1

   A.   mixed with peanuts

   B.   roasted over a fire

   C.   buttered and salted

   D.   coated with molasses

5. Which sentence from the article is an opinion?   I.C.11

   A.   Maize made up eighty percent of the Amerindian diet.

   B.   Peanuts and popcorn launched the snack food industry.

   C.   Native Americans brought popcorn to the first Thanksgiving.

   D.   Now, every American loves eating freshly popped popcorn.

6. Why did the popcorn business thrive during the Great Depression?   I.C.4

   A.   Television was not popular.

   B.   Candy was difficult to find.

   C.   Popcorn was an affordable treat.

   D.   Movie theaters gave it to customers.

7. Which is the best summary of the article?   I.C.1

   A.   Popcorn played an important role in ancient Aztec ceremonies.

   B.   Television replaced movies as the favored form of entertainment.

   C.   If European explorers had not seen Amerindians, we wouldn't have popcorn today

   D.   Popcorn has been used and eaten in a variety of ways for more than 80,000 years.

8. Read the following sentence from paragraph 8 of this article.

I.C.14

Americans today consume 17 billion quarts of popcorn each year.

The author included this information to show

A. popcorn is measured in quarts.
B. popcorn is still a popular snack.
C. popcorn is still available in America.
D. popcorn is no longer used as decoration.

Two men try to survive a very cold winter. Read what happens. Then answer questions 9 – 16. For some questions, you'll refer to certain paragraphs. Some questions refer to certain paragraphs. The paragraphs are numbered on the left side of the passage.

excerpt from *In A Far Country* by Jack London

1   As the sugar-pile and other little luxuries dwindled, they began to be afraid they were not getting their proper shares, and in order that they might not be robbed, they fell to gorging themselves. The luxuries suffered in this gluttonous contest, as did also the men.

2   In the absence of fresh vegetables and exercise, their blood became impoverished, and a loathsome, purplish rash crept over their bodies. Yet they refused to heed the warning.

3   Next, their muscles and joints began to swell, the flesh turning black, while their mouths, gums, and lips took on the color of rich cream. Instead of being drawn together by their misery, each gloated over the other's symptoms as the scurvy took its course.

4   They lost all regard for personal appearance, and for that matter, common decency. The cabin became a pigpen, and never once were the beds made or fresh pine boughs laid underneath. Yet they could not keep to their blankets, as they would have wished; for the frost was inexorable, and the fire box consumed much fuel. The hair of their heads and faces grew long and shaggy, while their garments would have disgusted a ragpicker. But they did not care. They were sick, and there was no one to see; besides, it was very painful to move about.

5   To all this was added a new trouble — the Fear of the North. This Fear was the joint child of the Great Cold and the Great Silence, and was born in the darkness of December, when the sun dipped below the horizon for good. It affected them according to their natures.

6   Weatherbee fell prey to the grosser superstitions, and did his best to resurrect the spirits which slept in the forgotten graves. It was a fascinating thing, and in his dreams they came to him from out of the cold, and snuggled into his blankets, and told him of their toils and troubles ere they died. He <u>shrank</u> away from the clammy contact as they drew closer and twined their frozen limbs about him, and when they whispered in his ear of things to come, the cabin rang with his frightened shrieks. Cuthfert did not understand — for they no longer spoke — and when thus awakened he invariably grabbed for his revolver. Then he would sit up in bed, shivering nervously, with the weapon trained on the unconscious dreamer. Cuthfert deemed the man going mad, and so came to fear for his life.

7   His own malady assumed a less concrete form. The mysterious artisan who had laid the cabin, log by log, had pegged a wind-vane to the ridgepole. Cuthfert noticed it always pointed south, and one day, irritated by its steadfastness of purpose, he turned it toward the east. He watched eagerly, but never a breath came by to disturb it. Then he turned the vane to the north, swearing never again to touch it till the wind did blow. But the air frightened him with its unearthly calm, and he often rose in the middle of the night to see if the vane had veered — ten degrees would have satisfied him. But no, it poised above him as unchangeable as fate.

9. In paragraph 1 the word <u>gluttonous</u> means   I.B.2

  A.   sugar coating.

  B.   rich looking.

  C.   excessive eating.

  D.   expensive dining.

10. What caused the men's scurvy?   I.C.4

  A.   a poor diet

  B.   a purple rash

  C.   poor hygiene

  D.   cold weather

11. In paragraph 4, when the author writes, "The cabin became a pigpen," what does he mean?   I.D.4

  A.   The men moved outside.

  B.   Pigs moved into the cabin.

  C.   The cabin was dirty and messy.

  D.   Weatherbee dreamed about pigs.

12. Why didn't the men stay in bed?   I.C.4

  A.   It was too painful to stay still.

  B.   They did not want to stay in bed.

  C.   They were frightened by their dreams.

  D.   They needed to keep feeding the fire.

13. In paragraph 6, the word <u>shrank</u> means   I.B.3

  A.   became smaller.

  B.   lessened in value.

  C.   pulled back instinctively.

  D.   to lose substance or weight.

14. Why did Cuthfert grab a gun when Weatherbee shrieked?   I.D.3

  A.   He was afraid Weatherbee might kill him.

  B.   He thought he heard the wind move the vane.

  C.   He thought someone was breaking into the cabin

  D.   He wanted to kill the spirits haunting Weatherbee.

15. What is the main idea of paragraph 7?   I.C.1

  A.   The cabin was built by an unknown man.

  B.   A wind vane on the house pointed north.

  C.   Cuthfert checked the vane day and night.

  D.   Cuthfert is frightened by the lack of wind.

Please write the answer to question 16 in your answer book.

16. Compare the Fear of the North's effect on Weatherbee and Cuthfert. Include specific details.   I.C.11

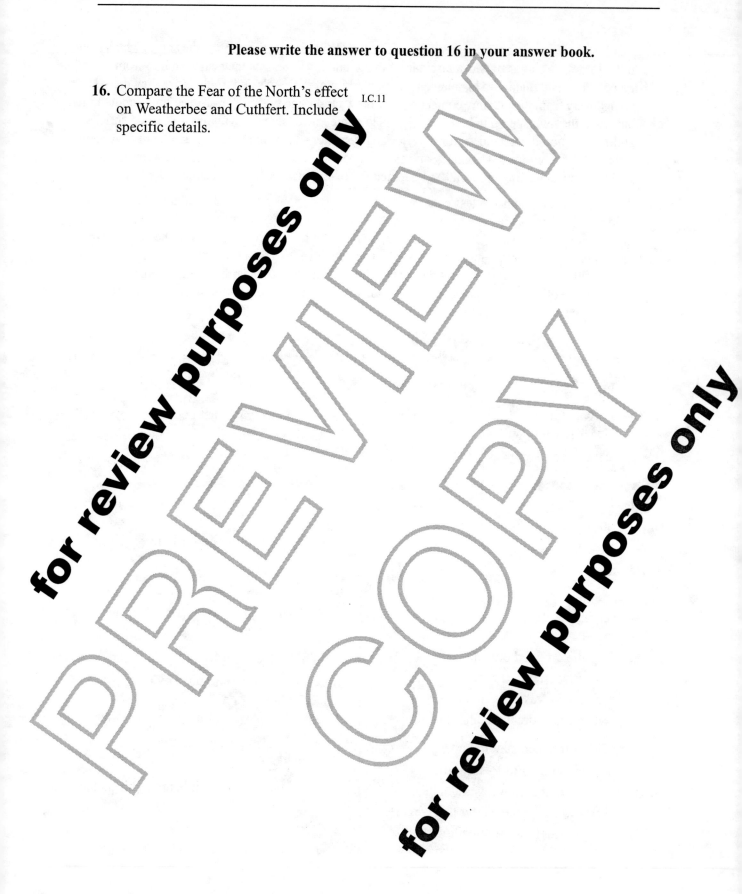

Segment 2

> Who is Jamal Amer Sayed? Read about his unique survival in modern Iraq. Then answer
> questions 17 – 25. Some questions may ask you about certain paragraphs. The paragraphs
> are numbered on the left side of the passage.

22 Years in Confinement

1   He lived in a drab, dirt and chamber three feet wide, by seven feet long, illuminated by only a single light bulb or a kerosene lantern. He created a living space and a seating platform out of dirt. He dug a hole deep enough to allow him to stand completely upright to bathe. He remained in this solitary confinement by choice for 22 years!

2   Jawad Amer Sayed was a follower of the Dawa party, one of Iraq's oldest opposition parties. During the revolution in Iraq, Dawa challenged the Baath Party regime. The Dawa killed numerous party officials and attempted to kill Saddam Hussein several times during the late 1970s and early 1980s.

3   In 1980, Saddam declared membership in Dawa a crime punishable by death. Thousands of members faced execution or fled the country.

4   In 1981, after learning Saddam Hussein's secret police executed two of his Dawa friends, Sayed went into exile. With only his mother, younger brother and two sisters knowing he was alive and well, he confined himself within the wall of his home. One word of his existence could mean capture, so only blood relatives could know his location. In Iraqi society, only these relatives could be trusted with deep family secrets.

5   Everyone else believed him to be dead. The police came looking for him twice, but to no avail. Once, his mother threw herself in front of a backhoe when a neighbor tried to build a cesspool too close to the hiding place. To protect his secret, his mother sent one of the sisters away from home to live with other relatives.

6   Sayed built the tiny living quarters in one night, fashioning a thin trap door entrance under a bed. A vent allowed air to filter in from the roof and a pipe drained water to the outside. He installed a toilet at one end of the compartment. A small peephole gave Sayed a view to the outside world. A small battery-operated radio kept him current with all the news, his favorite programs being from the British Broadcasting Corporation.

7   During his time of confinement, he lost weight, teeth, and even height. He grew a beard. While hiding, he memorized the Muslim holy book, The Koran. He even practiced calligraphy to while away the time.

8   For nourishment, Sayed ate rice and beans he cooked on a hot plate in the little room; his mother provided him with fruits and vegetables through the secret door.

179

9   Living south of Baghdad, he heard the bombing during the war. His home was near an ammunition depot and an air base.

10   On April 10, 2003, one day after Hussein fell from power in Iraq, Sayed exited his small hideaway, hardly able to walk and began living as a free man. He is now 49 years old and a mere skeleton of a man. Before going into hiding, he had studied management, now he would like to work if his health permits. He is enjoying looking at the stars and considers that hidden room his second home.

17. The author most likely wrote the passage to   I.C.14

   A. inform readers about Sayed's life.
   B. entertain readers with an adventure.
   C. persuade readers to join the Baath Party.
   D. explain to readers the risks of hiding in a wall.

18. Where did Sayed hide?   I.C.1

   A. under a dirt platform
   B. in his cousin's house
   C. inside the wall of his house
   D. under a neighbor's cesspool

19. Why did Sayed go into hiding?   I.D.3

   A. He was protecting his friend.
   B. He feared he would be killed.
   C. He was hiding from neighbors.
   D. He wanted to study the Koran.

20. Read the following sentence from paragraph 4 of the passage.   I.D.1

   In Iraqi society, only these relatives could be trusted with deep family secrets.

   The author included this information to show

   A. Sayed knew a family secret.
   B. Sayed lived by a set of rules.
   C. Sayed told secrets to his family.
   D. Sayed lived in extreme danger.

21. Why was one of Sayed's sisters sent away?   I.C.4

   A. to protect Sayed's secret
   B. to protect Sayed's sister
   C. so there would be enough food for Sayed
   D. because Sayed's mother was weak and ill

22. How did Sayed get air into his quarters?   I.C.

   A. through a thin trap door
   B. through a vent in the roof
   C. through a small peephole
   D. through a pipe to the outside

23. Read the following line from paragraph 10.   I.D.4

   He is now 49 years old and a mere skeleton of a man.

   The phrase skeleton of a man, means

   A. he has no spirit.
   B. he has no plan.
   C. he is very sad.
   D. he is very thin.

24. Sayed would most likely agree with which statement?   I.D.3

   A. Patience is overrated.
   B. Freedom is a great gift.
   C. Trust in no one but yourself.
   D. Do not hide from your enemies.

25. Which is the best summary of the passage?   I.C.1

- **A.** A man named Sayed proved it is possible to live inside a wall of a house.
- **B.** The Dawa party opposed the work and philosophy of the Baath Party.
- **C.** Sayed survived political persecution by hiding inside the wall of his house.
- **D.** Sayed's mother helped him hide by providing food and keeping his secret.

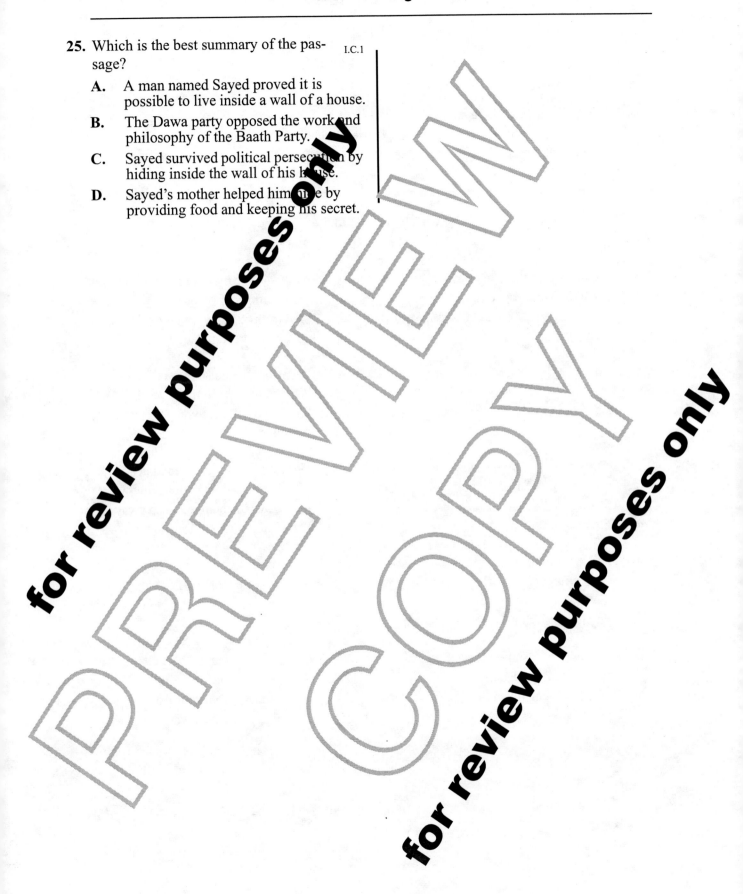

Segment 3

Strange events can occur in a big old house. Read about this poet's experiences. Then answer questions 26 – 32. Some questions refer to specific stanzas. The stanzas are numbered on the left side of the passage.

The Fearful Traveller in the Haunted Castle
George Moses Horton (1798? – 1880)

1 Often do I hear those windows open
And shut with dread surprise,
And spirits murmur and they grope,
But break not on the eyes.

2 Still <u>fancy</u> spies the winding sheet,
The phantom and the shroud,
And bids the pulse of horror beat
Throughout my ears aloud.

3 Some unknown finger thumps the door,
From one of faltering voice,
Till some one seems to walk the floor
With an alarming noise.

4 The drum of horror holds her sound,
Which will not let me sleep,
When ghastly breezes float around,
And hidden goblins creep.

5 Methinks I hear some constant groan,
The din of all the dead,
While trembling thus I lie alone
Upon this restless bed.

6 At length the blaze of morning broke
On my impatient view,
And truth or fancy told the joke,
And bade the night adieu.

7 'Twas but the noise of prowling rats,
Which ran with all their speed,
Pursued in haste by hungry cats,
Which on the <u>vermin</u> feed.

8 The cat growl'd as she held her prey,
Which shriek'd with all its might,
And drove the balm of sleep away
Throughout the live-long night.

9 Those creatures crumbling off the cheese
Which on the table lay;
Some cats too quick the rogues to seize,
With rumbling lost their prey.

10 Thus man is often his own elf,
Who makes the night his ghost,
And shrinks with horror from himself,
Which is to fear the most

–Courtesy Academic Affairs Library
University of North Carolina
Chapel Hill

26. The poet uses onomatopoeia to help the reader   I.D.7
    A. see the castle.
    B. hear the sounds.
    C. read with rhythm.
    D. know the speaker.

27. In stanza 7, the word <u>vermin</u> means   I.B.2
    A. rats.   C. ghosts.
    B. cats.   D. cheese.

28. What is the main idea of stanza 1?   I.C.
    A. The speaker opens a window to look for the spirits.
    B. The speaker can feel spirits reaching out and touching him.
    C. The speaker thinks he can hear spirits but cannot see them.
    D. The speaker is a spirit passing through an open castle window.

29. What is the main conflict in the poem?   I.D.12
    A. person versus fate
    B. person versus self
    C. person versus nature
    D. person versus person

30. Which is the best summary of the poem?   I.C.1
    A. Rats, spirits, and goblins live inside a haunted castle.
    B. The cats are very noisy as they chase and catch the rats.
    C. The speaker's imagination pictures ghosts and goblins in the night, but sees the actual cause of noise in the morning.
    D. Many strange and frightening things occur in a castle being haunted by ghosts and goblins in the middle of the night.

31. As it is used in stanza 2, the word <u>fancy</u> means   I.B.
    A. imagination.   C. eyes.
    B. reality.   D. elaborate.

Write the answer to question 32 in your answer book.

32. Explain how the author's mind tricks him into thinking his house is haunted. Give two examples from the poem.   I.D.12

Do daddy-long-legs bite? Read about these unusual arthropods. Then answer questions 33 – 39. For some questions, refer to certain paragraphs. The paragraphs are numbered on the left side of the passage.

Daddy-Long-Legs - Friends or Foes

1 I have many fond memories of playing with daddy-long-legs as a child. My own experiences cause me to be totally perplexed by other people's reactions to the little critters. For example, last year, I scared the wits out of a player at football practice simply by dangling one of my long-legged buddies three inches from his nose. The unexpected visitor would have delighted me. However, the quarterback screamed like a starving baby He even refused to speak to me for the rest of the school year. Why would anyone react that way to a daddy-long-legs?

2 I received the answer this year when my friend started speaking to me again. It seems that my friend, like many others, confused my daddy-long-legs with the cellar spider. Since people frequently confuse the two creatures, scientists often refer to the cellar spider as the daddy-long-legs spider. Additionally, my friend assumed all spiders had a poisonous bite. Neither of these assumptions is correct.

3 The daddy-long-legs is not a true spider. It is an arthropod. Arthropods are in the same class with spiders but not the same order. Everyone knows arthropods are much more interesting than spiders. Both the real daddy-long-legs and its namesake, the daddy-long-legs spider, have eight long legs. However, a close inspection reveals major differences. The daddy-long-legs has a single-segment body with two tiny eyes. The spider has a body with two segments, eight eyes, and fangs.

4 Of course, many people might not want to get that up close and personal with a spider. Fortunately, watching the two creatures' behavior from a polite distance may actually tell you more. Daddy-long-legs like to hang out under logs or rocks. You might even spot one using its long flexible legs to crawl over a raspberry bush or up a cabin wall. The spider prefers life in a dark corner of a basement. While daddy-long-legs dine on plant juices, the spider will catch moths, flies, and any other insects that fly or crawl in your basement. The spider's victims become its dinner. The daddy-long-legs cannot produce silk, but its namesake spins sticky, stringy webs with its silk.

5 Daddy-long-legs don't bite and daddy-long-legs spiders, unlike many other spiders, can't break skin. Therefore, you have no reason to panic whether it is a real daddy-long-legs or a daddy-long-legs spider. Remember this the next time you see a daddy-long-legs and don't run for the hills. There is much more to these fascinating creatures than their eight long spindly legs.

33. Which of the following statements best reflects the theme of the passage?   I.C.14

   A. Don't judge a book by its cover.

   B. Real courage comes from within.

   C. A rose by any other name is still a rose.

   D. The apple doesn't fall far from the tree.

34. Which phrase from the passage contains a simile?   I.D.7

   A. the unexpected visitor

   B. my long-legged buddies

   C. scared the wits out of a player

   D. screamed like a starving baby

35. Which statement from the passage is an opinion?   I.C.11

   A. He even refused to speak to me for the rest of the school year.

   B. The real daddy-long-legs is not a true spider. It is an arthropod.

   C. The daddy-long-legs has a single segment body with two tiny eyes.

   D. Everyone knows arthropods are much more interesting than spiders.

36. Why was the speaker confused by her friend's reaction to the daddy-long-legs?   I.C.4

   A. The speaker thought football players were fearless.

   B. The speaker knew the facts about daddy-long-legs.

   C. The speaker did not know there was a cellar spider.

   D. The speaker had never before seen a similar reaction.

37. The reader can conclude that the author most likely believes   I.C.4

   A. spiders make great pets.

   B. everyone has a basement.

   C. daddy-long-legs are harmless.

   D. cellar spiders can be dangerous.

38. Which detail sentence would best support the main idea of paragraph 5?   I.C.1

   A. My football friend no longer fears spiders.

   B. People have become very ill from spider bites.

   C. I have studied the behavior of daddy-long-legs since I was seven years old.

   D. The daddy-long-legs spider carries venom, but it can't get the venom into you.

39. The author wrote this article most likely to   I.D.12

   A. eliminate people's fear of daddy-long-legs.

   B. describe the habitats of spiders and insects.

   C. suggest new ways to frighten your friends.

   D. explain that many people have unusual fears.

Segment 4

Does losing weight require dietary supplements? Read what one author says about this subject. Then answer questions 41-48. Some questions may ask you about certain paragraphs. The paragraphs are numbered on the left side of the passage.

Dietary Supplements: Beyond the Label

1 Advertisements for dietary supplements bombard consumers. It is impossible to turn on the television, open a magazine, or surf the Web without seeing an ad for these products. This daily dose of <u>media</u> advertising sells vitamin and mineral supplements. Additionally, they market products to increase energy, improve athletic performance, or aid in weight loss. How truthful are these claims, and how safe are these products?

2 Many dietary supplements seem to improve health and well-being. They may contain, among other things, vitamins, minerals, herbs, and botanicals. However, many dietary supplements are ineffective. Others are worse than ineffective. They cause real harm and even contribute to death. For example, supplements containing ephedra were linked to serious health outcomes such as heart attack and stroke.

3 How can consumers protect themselves against misleading ads about such supplements? By thinking critically about the information, asking questions, and performing research, you can evaluate the information and make smart decisions. Start by asking yourself some basic questions. Is the claim too good to be true? Is this an article or an ad?

4 As you flip through a magazine and read about someone who has quickly lost one hundred pounds or can suddenly lift twice his body weight, ponder the source. One such weight loss ad had gullible shoppers lined up waiting to buy the product. In fact, many of my personal friends and close relatives bought into that outrageous claim. I advised them to ask one important question: did an unbiased medical expert write this claim or a paid advertising expert? Make sure any claim made has solid scientific data supporting it.

5 Many stores stock their shelves with a wide variety of dietary supplements. Everyone believes all products sold in a health food store must be good for you. However, the only reason a health food store sells supplements is to make lots of money. All of the store managers know none of these products are good for you.

6 The good news is that you are not in this situation completely alone. The Food and Drug Administration investigates complaints against dangerous products. Once they can prove the harmful effects of the supplements, they can ban the product. For example, the FDA banned supplements containing ephedra in February 2004, after learning of the critically ill effects it had on dieters. The bad news is supplement companies do not need the approval of the Food and Drug Administration before putting their product on the market. The consumer plays the role of the lab rat. The product on the shelf might be completely safe, or it just may not have done enough damage yet to gain the attention of the FDA.

7 Along with evaluating the product, evaluate your reason for purchasing it. What is your goal for the supplement? The smiling models who jog, ride bikes, or just lounge in swimsuits in the ads draw many customers to the products. The wise consumer knows popping a supplement won't turn you into one of those models. Evaluate your goal. Is it realistic? Could you skip the supplements and achieve that goal with a balanced diet and regular exercise? Will meeting that goal improve your life and overall health? When in doubt, ask a doctor or other healthcare provider for advice.

40. In paragraph 1, the word <u>media</u> means   I.B.2

   A.   claims.

   B.   consumer.

   C.   mass communication.

   D.   vitamins and minerals.

41. The author most likely wrote this article for   I.C.14

   A.   doctors.

   B.   shoppers.

   C.   advertising executives.

   D.   supplement manufacturers.

42. Read the following sentences from the article.   I.C.6

   > Others are worse than ineffective. They cause real harm and even contribute to death.

   What evidence does the author give to support these statements?

   A.   Supplements containing ephedra, were linked to serious health outcomes such as heart attack and stroke.

   B.   The smiling models who jog, ride bikes, or just lounge in swimsuits in the ads draw many customers to the products.

   C.   In fact, many of my personal friends and close relatives bought into that outrageous claim.

   D.   The wise consumer knows popping a supplement won't turn you into one of those models.

43. What was the purpose for taking ephedra supplements?   I.C.4

   A.   to gain strength

   B.   to fight colds

   C.   to reduce weight

   D.   to improve vision

44. Which statement in paragraph 5 is a fact?   I.C.11

   A.   Many stores stock their shelves with a wide variety of dietary supplements.

   B.   Everyone believes all products sold in a health food store must be good for you.

   C.   The only reason a health food store sells supplements is to make lots of money.

   D.   All of the store managers know none of these products are good for you.

45. The author most likely believes makers of supplements use unproven claims because   I.C.4

   A.   the facts are boring.

   B.   they increase sales.

   C.   people enjoy reading them.

   D.   they believe them to be true.

46. What propaganda technique does the author use that shows her bias in the article?   I.C.6

   A.   loaded words

   B.   snob appeal

   C.   bandwagon statements

   D.   unreliable testimony

47. Which best reflects the theme of this article? I.C.14

    A. Look before you leap.

    B. True friends are a gift.

    C. Honesty is the best policy.

    D. Penny wise, pound foolish.

Write the answer to question 48 in your answer book.

48. Summarize the steps the author recommends to evaluate claims in ads. I.C.1

American Book Company
The Standards Experts

Grade 9 Writing, MCA-II, MCA-III, BST, ACT

Please fill out the form completely, and return by mail or fax to American Book Company.

Purchase Order #: _____   Date: _____

Contact Person: _____

School Name (and District, if any): _____
_____

Billing Address: _____   Street Address: ☐ same as billing
_____   _____

Attn: _____   Attn: _____
_____   _____
_____   _____

Phone: _____ E-Mail: _____

Credit Card #: _____ Exp Date: _____

Authorized Signature: _____

Order Number	Product Title	Pricing* (30 books)	Qty	Pricing (30 e-books)	Qty	Pricing (30 books + 30 e-books)	Qty	Total Cost
MN6-M0211	Mastering the MN 6th Grade MCA-III Mathematics Test	$388.50 (1 set of 30 books)		$388.50 (1 set of 30 e-books)		$717.00 (30 books+ 30 e-books)		
MN7-M1110	Mastering the MN 7th Grade MCA-III Mathematics Test	$388.50 (1 set of 30 books)		$388.50 (1 set of 30 e-books)		$717.00 (30 books+ 30 e-books)		
MN8-M0410	Passing the MN 8th Grade MCA-III Mathematics Test	$388.50 (1 set of 30 books)		$388.50 (1 set of 30 e-books)		$717.00 (30 books+ 30 e-books)		
MN8-R0906	Passing the MN 8th Grade MCA-II Reading Test	$388.50 (1 set of 30 books)		$388.50 (1 set of 30 e-books)		$717.00 (30 books+ 30 e-books)		
MN9-W0406	Passing the MN Grade 9 Test of Written Composition	$388.50 (1 set of 30 books)		$388.50 (1 set of 30 e-books)		$717.00 (30 books+ 30 e-books)		
MN-M0410	Passing the MN MCA-II/GRAD Component Math Test REVISED	$388.50 (1 set of 30 books)		$388.50 (1 set of 30 e-books)		$717.00 (30 books+ 30 e-books)		
MN-R0406	Passing the MN MCA-II/GRAD Component Reading Test	$388.50 (1 set of 30 books)		$388.50 (1 set of 30 e-books)		$717.00 (30 books+ 30 e-books)		
MN-M1104	Passing the MN Basic Skills Test in Mathematics	$388.50 (1 set of 30 books)		$388.50 (1 set of 30 e-books)		$717.00 (30 books+ 30 e-books)		
MN-R0899	Passing the MN Basic Skills Test in Reading	$388.50 (1 set of 30 books)		$388.50 (1 set of 30 e-books)		$717.00 (30 books+ 30 e-books)		
ACT-E0708	ACT English Test Preparation Guide	$299.70 (1 set of 30 books)		$299.70 (1 set of 30 e-books)		$539.40 (30 books+ 30 e-books)		
ACT-M0708	ACT Mathematics Test Preparation Guide	$329.70 (1 set of 30 books)		$329.70 (1 set of 30 e-books)		$599.40 (30 books+ 30 e-books)		
ACT-R0708	ACT Reading Test Preparation Guide	$299.70 (1 set of 30 books)		$299.70 (1 set of 30 e-books)		$539.40 (30 books+ 30 e-books)		
ACT-S0608	ACT Science Test Preparation Guide	$299.70 (1 set of 30 books)		$299.70 (1 set of 30 e-books)		$539.40 (30 books+ 30 e-books)		
ACT-W0711	ACT Writing Test Preparation Guide	$299.70 (1 set of 30 books)		$299.70 (1 set of 30 e-books)		$539.40 (30 books+ 30 e-books)		

8-1-11   *Minimum order is 1 set of 30 books of the same subject.

Subtotal _____

Shipping & Handling 12%
Shipping 6% on print and digital packages
Shipping waived on digital resources _____

Total _____

American Book Company ● PO Box 2638 ● Woodstock, GA 30188-1383
Toll Free Phone: 1-888-264-5877 ● Toll-Free Fax: 1-866-827-3240
Web Site: www.americanbookcompany.com

Call Toll-Free 1-888-264-5877 to ORDER and for FREE PREVIEW COPIES!

Visit americanbookcompany.com to download FREE SAMPLES of all of our products!